General Semantics Seminar 1937

Transcription of Notes From Lectures
in General Semantics
Given at Olivet College

By

Alfred Korzybski

Third Edition
Edited by Homer J. Moore, Jr.

Institute of General Semantics
Brooklyn, New York

General Semantics Seminar 1937, Third Edition
by Alfred Korzybski
Copyright © 2002 by Institute of General Semantics
First Edition 1937
Second Edition 1964, Edited by Edward L. Gates

All rights reserved. No part of this book may be reproduced or transmitted in any form or by any means, electronic or mechanial including photocopying, recording or any information storage or retrieval system without prior permission from the publisher, except for brief quotations in an article or review.

Publisher's Catalogue in Publication Data
Korzybski, Alfred
  General semantics seminar 1937 transcription of notes from lectures in general semantics given at Olivet College / Alfred Korzybski - Third ed.
  Institute of General Semantics © 2002
  xi, 237 p.
  ISBN 0-910780-15-3 (paperback: acid free paper)
  LC Card Number: 2002105268
  1. General semantics. 2. Applied Psychology. 3. Practical Philosophy. 4. Behavioral Science
  I. Title. II. Korzybski, Alfred

LC Classification # B820
Dewey Decimal Classification 149.94

Cover Design by Edward Dawson

If you would like more information on the Institute of General Semantics and its programs and publications, or would like to support its work with a contribution, please contact us:

Institute of General Semantics	Phone: 718-921-7093
86 85th Street	Fax: 718-921-4276
Brooklyn, New York 11209-4208	Email: institute@general-semantics.org
USA	Web: www.general-semantics.org

Leading a Revolution in Human Evaluating™

FOREWORD TO THE THIRD EDITION

Alfred Korzybski wrote *Manhood of Humanity* after his experiences in World War I. At that time, he posited that "the World War mark[ed] ... the end of Humanity's Childhood and the beginning of Humanity's Manhood". However, when I look around at the world's situation as we begin the Twenty-first Century, this seems too optimistic to me. Albanians, Croats, and Serbs are carrying on ethnic-based civil war in the Balkans. In the Middle East, the 'peace process' between the Palestinians and the Israelis seems to have totally broken down, with deaths on both sides occurring weekly. In Iraq, Kurdish and Shi'ite populations face military attacks, and Saddam Hussein continues to make threatening moves against Kuwait, Saudi Arabia, and the U.S. planes patrolling the "no-fly zone". In Africa, Rebels from the southern portion of Sudan fight government troops from the north, while AIDS and famine affect most of the continent. In the United States, in the two years since the Columbine Shooting, over forty school shooting incidents have occurred. Etc., etc. It seems to me that we have entered the "Teen-hood of Humanity", at best.

It seems evident to me that the need for Korzybski's insights has never been greater. In light of this, the Institute of General Semantics presents this new edition of the transcript of the seminar Korzybski gave at Olivet College in 1937. In this early presentation, he gives a complete outline of his system with the training methods needed to apply it. This seminar makes an excellent starting point for those wishing to apply general semantics in their daily lives.

We have made few modifications in this edition. Most of them were to conform with current IGS usage policy, or for consistency. Korzybski's style has been preserved. We hope that you will find this presentation both useful and entertaining.

Help towards this edition was provided by Susan Presby Kodish who proofread the manuscript. Jeff Mordkowitz, Director of the Institute of General Semantics, provided editorial consultation.

Homer J. Moore

Manchaca, Texas
May 2001

EDITOR'S NOTE

Abbreviated notes from Alfred Korzybski's 1937 Seminar in General Semantics at Olivet College, Michigan, were reproduced that year and distributed by the Olivet College Book Store.

The notes had been transcribed by Keith Ball, then a student of history at Olivet. Korzybski roughly revised some of the manuscript, but did not read the final version before publication. The 1937 printing was titled *General Semantics* and is listed as Item 15 in the 'Bibliography of the Writings of Alfred Korzybski' in *General Semantics Bulletin* No. 3, 1950.

The first move toward republication of the seminar notes was made after Guthrie E. Janssen compiled *Selections from Science and Sanity* (published 1948), when he started editing them. When Janssen left the Institute the project was set aside, temporarily.

In finally presenting *Seminar 1937*, we are particularly hopeful those who read it will also be serious students of *Science and Sanity*. Korzybski's spoken presentation, which delighted hundreds of seminar students over the years, was not carefully worked over as was his writing and we have not tried to polish it editorially.

Help toward this 1964 printing has been given by Mrs. Chelie Miller, who typed the manuscript, and Ken Mansuy, who helped proofread. Charlotte S. Read, literary executor of Alfred Korzybski, and M. Kendig, Director of the Institute of General Semantics, have contributed substantially and patiently.

Edward L Gates

Lime Rock, Connecticut
November 1964

FOREWORD TO THE SECOND EDITION

My acquaintance with General Semantics began about 1930 when Alfred Korzybski submitted a large part of the manuscript of *Science and Sanity* to the publishing house with which I was then connected. I struggled through the carbon copy on onionskin paper of this unrevised version with mounting excitement. Although after discussion with my colleagues, we decided that as a young firm devoted so far largely to literature and the fine arts, we had neither the facilities nor the know-how to undertake the publication of a work of this sort, it nonetheless marked the beginning for me of a long and close friendship with Alfred Korzybski.

When in 1935 I found myself at Olivet College in Michigan and Korzybski was in Chicago, it was natural for me to want him to come to Olivet. This he did on several occasions. We arranged in the first instance that he should give two introductory lectures and practically the whole, small college community turned out to hear them. The reactions varied from anger through confusion to enthusiasm but there was no indifference.

This acted as a sort of ferment in the institution and when two years later, Korzybski undertook to conduct an extended seminar of fourteen sessions at the College, the attendance, which was entirely voluntary, was surprisingly large. This, I believe, was one of the first of the long series later conducted under the auspices of the Institute which was founded the next year. Arrangements were made to have the lectures taken down stenographically and the transcription was then roughly revised by Korzybski for publication. Those who have attended later seminars will recognize the basic pattern that was set here. Korzybski sought constantly to refine and improve and enrich the presentation to make it more effective, and to adapt it to the particular group present, but the fundamental method and content are here.

Re-reading the Olivet Seminar now, it is extraordinary to find how the rhythm, tone and flavor of Korzybski come through. To those who knew him, it is easy in going through this text to visualize his gestures and especially his mobile features, the quizzical expression succeeded by a warm, broad smile, his eyes shifting quickly from an amused twinkle to a penetrating intensity. But these nostalgic reminders aside, it is important to have these lectures available again for they are basic documents in the development of General Semantics.

Joseph Brewer

Paul Klapper Library, Queens College
Flushing, New York, October 1963

GENERAL SEMANTICS SEMINAR 1937

CONTENTS

Foreword to the Third Edition	iii
Editor's Note	v
Foreword to the Second Edition	vii
Preface (1937)	x
Lecture One	1
Lecture Two	17
Lecture Three	33
Lecture Four	51
Lecture Five	73
Lecture Six	87
Lecture Seven	101
Lecture Eight	113
Lecture Nine	129
Lecture Ten	143
Lecture Eleven	155
Lecture Twelve	169
Lecture Thirteen	187
Lecture Fourteen	205
Supplement: A Semantic Interpretation of the Fundamental Values in the Study of Foreign Languages	227
Addenda for 1964 Edition: Two 1937 letters from Joseph Brewer	230, 231

PREFACE (1937)

Science and Sanity: An Introduction to Non-aristotelian Systems and General Semantics was published in the autumn of 1933, introducing General Semantics to the public (General Theory of Values). Since then co-workers have *applied* extensionalization to 'mentally' ill, in hospitals and private psychiatric practice; reformatories; education, both of abnormal and 'normal' persons in some schools, colleges and universities; and finally in private adjustment of the individual lives of different lay students. General Semantics has also been utilized by specialists in various branches of science to revise the older formulations and difficulties. Some of the experimental results have been reported before the *First American Congress for General Semantics*, held, March 1 and 2, 1935, at Washington State Normal School, Ellensburg, Washington, in various scientific papers, and also in correspondence with the writer. The results seem uniform and standard; namely, that 'extensionalization' is in principle, workable when applied in practice. Some of the results are: (1) After a few months training some 'mental' cases recovered, without relapses thus far; (2) subnormal students became practically 'average'; (3) some of the poorest students became the best; (4) students overcame unclassified blockages and handicaps, became better adjusted to life and found their studies easier; (5) practically in 99 per cent of cases, in *serious students* of General Semantics, some individual beneficial results in adjustment followed; (6) a number of psychiatrists report that they find semantic methods efficient in shortening the period of psychotherapy, allowing also for group treatment; (7) the writer in his seminars has verified these seemingly automatic general results.

In conclusion it may be stated that the white race[*] has come to an impasse, the *actual* conditions of life are shaped by *extensional* science; while our inner orientations and the structure of language remain intensional. Increasing maladjustments must follow, as we actually observe. Future issues are clear from the point of view of *predictability*, either we return to primitive states and abolish extensional science, and then perhaps survive; or we transform our orientations to conform with the actualities of our lives, in other words extensionalize them. It seems that this choice must be made as a general cultural issue and we must stop reading animal and primitive reactions into the white man and by extensional scientific analysis find out what standards of evaluation belong to the white man's level and correspond to the functioning of his nervous system. In General Semantics such an attempt has been made, and so far results seem to justify it.

An extract from "Neuro-Semantic and Neuro-Linguistic Mechanisms of Extensionalization, General Semantics as a Natural Experimental Science" by Alfred Korzybski. Paper presented before the Psychology Section, A.A.A.S., St. Louis, December 1935. Reprinted from *American Journal of Psychiatry*, Volume 93, Number 1, July 1936.

---

[*] See footnote on page 5.

SEMINAR LECTURE ONE

To begin with, lose all fear. You know in Dante's Inferno there was an inscription, "Lose all hope; you who enter here". I would have on the door of a class in General Semantics*, "Get all hope; you who enter". We have to get acquainted to begin with. Lose your tension about these seminars. We will be at home; we will be very chummy. If you don't understand something, tell me and I will repeat it, endlessly. Don't have the feeling either that you are students and that I am a teacher. No. You are human beings, $Smith_1$, $Smith_2$, $Smith_3$, etc. — and so I am, say, $Smith_n$. Human beings talking to human beings. Relax to begin with. Don't take it too dramatically.

I will say a lot about mathematics and psychiatry; two subjects that you know are very unpopular. The reason why I will speak a lot *about* mathematics is because mathematics is the simplest language. I will ask you simple questions and I will want you to respond to them. If you do not understand something tell me, for we must work together. You as a group, if I do not speak loudly enough tell me so. Let's be at home. If you want me to repeat something tell me so. Heckling I will not tolerate

---

* For convenience, hereafter *General Semantics* will be abbreviated GS.

for the simple reason that the heckler is often too brilliant a verbalist to be intelligent. Cheap brilliance is not a working intelligence. But, I want to cooperate with my students, have you get what I have to say, and this, as your President Brewer once said, is very simple but not easy.

Sometimes I am ashamed to lecture on my subject, and the reason for it is — as I call it — that it is so idiotically simple; and yet it is one of the most difficult things I know to acquire, and yet idiotically simple. I want to disperse a sort of attitude particularly among students that GS is extraordinarily difficult. You so often say, "Something is above my head". Well, nothing is above our heads, but sometimes the presentation of a subject is so unsatisfactory that it makes simple things difficult. This applies to classes in schools, colleges, and universities. Of course, teachers have to know something about the art of presentation. I remember there was a girl in a school where I was lecturing on extensionalization, who particularly disliked mathematics. Her teacher was at my seminar and the girl was surprised when I told her that her teacher was not clear. Before long she lost all dislike for mathematics and began to like it. High grade teachers are needed if one is to do a high grade piece of work. In this college you are lucky in this way. You have an excellent staff and a very forward looking President. What in the dickens is the value of education? Why all this work? Preparing for a career? Would you prefer a son with a profession and a salary who is unhappy, to one without the profession but who is happy? The whole aim of education is to prepare the student for life and the older education does not do that. They prepare automatons. Life is something more than a profession. In this particular college you are lucky that they are looking for you to be prepared for life. In trying to make dry technicians out of you education fails. Preparing for life is the supreme aim of education, as a 'profession' is only a part of life. We are making every kind of educational experiments. Most of them are quite silly; but what happens? Do you know? You will get old and die before they will know their experiments were not scientifically modern. Should education not inquire scientifically what is the foundation of education? Why do we not do this? Because most educators are very ignorant of mathematics and exact sciences. In GS we coordinate science and education, and life and sanity.

I will speak a great deal about mathematics and psychiatry. The reason for it is that in our human orientation, until now, the disciplines were carried for their own sakes. They were worked by themselves; and the methodological findings did not affect our general orientations.

Tell me what would you do if you had a bad cavity in your tooth. You would consult a dentist, wouldn't you? Well, how about if you have a very bad cavity in your adjustment. Would it not be right to consult a 'mental' specialist? Yes. Why, if you have trouble in your adjustment, do you not consult a specialist? Is your brain and brain product, otherwise[1] your own orientation, less important than the color of your urine? Is it worthwhile to take care of your brains? I advise you definitely, as youth and a young generation, whenever you get in any kind of

---

[1] In this instance, and most of the following, Korzybski uses "otherwise" where I would say "in other words". [HJM]

difficulties in adjustment, to consult a specialist in psychiatry. It does not mean that you're insane. You see, we are living under a different set of semantic environments. The Mohammedans proclaimed the insane blessed; the Christians proclaimed them obsessed by the devil. You see, the difference between sanity and insanity is a question of degree. Similar mechanisms are found in asylums as well as in this class. The question is to know how to take care of them.

Speaking of psychiatry, I do not want you to think for a moment that I am implying anything about this class except that similar mechanisms work similarly in both, and the problems of adjustment to life and the whole problem of psychotherapy concentrate on the consciousness of the mechanism. In the old days we were not conscious of the mechanisms and the moment we get conscious of the mechanisms most of the problems become solved. Then the whole problem is to discover and get conscious of the mechanisms. Get conscious of what is going on in you. I will try to deliver the goods to every one of you so that you will each know wherein lies the trouble. Every one of us has some sort of problems and the question is to know how to solve these problems. All of you have had them and will have some more.

All of you have had training in algebra. The old way of looking at it was "science for science's sake". Today we should know better. Science exists only for the solution of human problems. Now imagine that you have *read* a book on algebra. All of you have handled a book like that no matter how much you got out of it. When you *read* the book only, could you solve a problem, by a mere reading of the book? No. What have you to do then to solve problems by algebra? You would have to get a drill in the technique of algebra. Reading a book will not help you. Algebra exists only for the solution of problems.

Now, in GS it is just like another kind of algebra; it exists and its only value is to help the solution of life's problems. But, we have to have a technique. You must master the technique before you can apply it and solve the problems. My only aim is to help you to solve your own problems. Often people ask me, "'There is a problem. How do you solve it?" It is not my business to solve your problems. It is my business to give you a *method* to *solve your own problems*. I cannot know your private problems with full ramifications, can I? Can I give you valid private opinions? Remember, private opinions are undependable. No one is entitled to their own private opinions. You have to supplement your private opinions by the opinions of the white race[2], which we call science. For, science is nothing but racial opinions. Have that attitude for racial opinions, it is the most authoritative, and

---

[2] Korzybski's references to "the white race" were made in the era of 1915-1940. In 2002 it may sound strange to speak in such terms. Some people have interpreted his comments on "the white race" as indicating racial prejudices. Korzybski's actual 'racial biases' were elucidated in *Science and Sanity* (page 404) where he wrote, "Practically all the vicious, unjustified, and unscientific generalizations which have made the white race the most animalistic, selfish, cruel, hypocritical, and un-sane race on earth are mainly due to the biological, [aristotelian], distorted reasonings and [semantic reactions] produced by false analogy." On page 406, he explained, "[I speak about] the white race [because] I do not know enough about the structures of languages of other races and their [semantic reactions] to speak about them."

the best thing we have to date. Private opinions are dangerous, but if they are backed by science, they acquire a certain probability. My stressing of mathematical method and psychiatry is due to the fact that in our general orientations we have completely disregarded these two. We carry them for their own sake but the wisdom we get from mathematics and psychiatry have never been applied to life. In GS and in human sciences we can not disregard scientific methodology. Human evaluation at its worst is called 'insanity'. Human evaluations at their best are found in mathematics and mathematical sciences. In GS we take mathematical methods and psychiatrical methods into consideration and apply them to our *general orientation*, something that has never been done before. Private opinions are worthless whether they are yours or mine. In my lectures I'll have to say often this is "my private opinion" to forewarn you of their probable invalidity. If private opinions are backed by *racial* opinions (science), which is nothing but opinion, then we know we have the best of 1937, and at least we have something to go by. Now, lets go to the foundations of what we call GS.

What is it all about? The term *semantics* is not new. It comes from a Greek word meaning "significance", "value", "meaning". It has been used many years ago, but the old semantics is now dead. I call this new discipline *General Semantics* to make a difference from the old use. The science of GS is the science of values — evaluation. A general science of values and evaluation. I want you to realize and evaluate this by yourselves because I cannot do that for you. In GS we deal with *values* and *evaluation*, which represent mighty problems.

I want you to realize that whenever you like something or when you dislike something, you love or hate, etc.; what are you inwardly *doing*? *Evaluating*! This is our most important problem and in GS "evaluation", "evaluating", "values" become *technical terms*. I will speak all through the seminars about the importance of using this term *evaluation*; there are endless problems involved in it. You will find that every psychological reaction is a *problem of evaluation*. Tonight we are only getting acquainted. I am not starting tonight the technical presentation. When we deal with a general theory of evaluation we are dealing at once with *every psychological* and sometimes even organic reactions in yourself. When you say you love or hate somebody, are you evaluating? Yes. Then when you say something about any of your feelings or orientations are you not dealing with the deepest evaluations? A general theory of evaluation including all your private and public and whatnot orientations cannot disregard science and mathematics as fundamental for the science of evaluation. In GS we treat evaluation in a general way. But get this much; that mathematics gives a theory of evaluation in a narrow sense.

In my seminars there is no difference between faculty and students. GS is so new that if an Einstein would be here among us, the course of lectures would not be changed. Your feelings are what I mean by evaluation. Evaluation turns out to be in GS a *technical* term. I will explain about this later. If you think about everything which happens to you in terms of evaluation instead of "loving", "hating", etc., then that is evaluation; and when we have investigated factors of evaluation, then we are getting a hold on what is going on in you. There is another connection with science and in particular mathematics and mathematical physics. This is predictability in mathematical sciences. We have predicted stars, etc.; mathematical predictability has allowed us to do this. But often when we have so predicted we look at the spot and there is no star, but later on they build up a better telescope and they find what was predicted, predicted by mathematics. This is one of the miracles of mathematics. Predictability. Now, fancy life if we could predict. Would we make some efforts, if we could predict, not to be happy with it? I do not need to go further. If we could predict some unhappy ending would we do it? Please get the importance of predictability. Is not that a foundation for human happiness? In GS we will investigate the principles of, and factors of, predictability. At present the maximum predictability does exist in mathematical sciences, etc. But happily, by applying those principles we can apply predictability to life. To do this would turn out to be very wise on the surface but on the bottom we are applying *only* factors of predictability, so our orientations become predictable and our adjustment becomes better. Now the question of predictability becomes a question of method. There are questions in mathematics that are more important than technicalities: namely the question of *method*. If we can discover this method, and also discover how this method applies to life, we are discovering the factors of predictability as applied to life. Then, if we could predict with any sort of certainty what will happen to us if we do so and so; we would do it, or we would not. This predictability applies even to wars: England and America participation in the World War, and German decision for war.

If we had any predictability would the world be in the situation it is now in? The question of method is a great deal more general than technical. Every one of you has had enough mathematics to know about the technical side of it, but none of us has had enough so as to know about the *methods*. GS being an advanced theory of values, a general theory of evaluation, all our psychological reactions turn out to be problems of evaluation. If we get hold of the factors of evaluation, we get hold of ourself and, in fact, of the other fellow. As the seminar develops you will see how it works. I want to emphasize that GS is strictly empirical; it is experimental. It does work as predicted.

GS has its application to psychiatry. Talking about psychiatry again, do not forget that we have prejudices against psychiatry that are unjustifiable, because each of us has similar mechanisms to the 'mentally' ill, it is only a question of degree. I stress the empirical character of GS and there is no question of speculation or a play on words. It deals with the nervous system which at present we abuse; and this prepares us for 'insanity'. Only when we get hold of those factors can we clear this up. There are elements in education and in so-called science that lead directly to 'insanity'.

We are training our children towards 'insanity'. I will show you how those factors operate even today in mathematics and physics. We are talking about the solution of human problems and I want to convey methods for the solution of sanity. We try to solve problems in sociology, economics, politics, etc., the most complex problems in existence; and yet do you know that in the great discipline of mathematics there are today two camps and they each call the other camp 'insane'? They have agreed to disagree, and that is the kind of 'beauty' even in mathematics. What can we say about our human affairs when we have such a mess even in mathematics and at the bottom of sciences? In GS we are not doing any cosmic legislation. We are clarifying linguistic issues and you will see what happens to any problem — very often clarify your language and there is no problem.

Do you want to know the origin of the American depression? It is a scandalous affair. After the War they had, in Washington, D. C., a conference between bankers, industrialists, labor, and scientists. The problem was to adjust future American affairs to meet the current after-war problems. They were all talking good English, but they could not understand each other at all. Just as if they had been Chinese and Japanese, they could not understand each other. The labor head got sick and tired of the 'whole mess' and he asked this question, "May I ask you a question? Does *yes* always mean *yes*, or sometimes does it mean *no*?" This threw the meeting into a panic and they adjourned, but a group of professors returned to the meeting some hours later and told the conference that "yes" always means "yes" and "no" always means "no". Of course, the whole conference failed because of the meaning of "yes" and "no", and the whole conference was disrupted because of this. You will see later how sometimes "yes" may mean "yes" or it might mean "no" depending on the question; but out of that verbalistic confusion grew the American depression.

You will find a lot of such issues, *verbal issues*, on which the fate of persons as well as nations depend. So the clarification of those issues is one of the most important questions man can face today. For we will find a great many problems are *no problems*, but that they are only *verbal messes*. Clear up these verbal messes and you clear up the 'problem'. I am not solving problems, but I am clearing up the verbal messes by investigating the structure of our language.

You are getting an understanding of how verbal misunderstanding in understanding can make messes out of questions. The League of Nations is a laughing-stock. Why? Because their actions involve verbal evaluations and linguistic difficulties. And in these there is *no predictability*. Have you gotten the private value of predictability? The value in your private life? If you could predict, would that be of value to you? Is it worthwhile to discover the factors of predictability? That is what we will be doing. We will be looking for factors of predictability. I want to stress one point, and there are no limits to what extent I want to stress this. What I may tell you is sometimes dramatic and often tragic. All I say, and you can ask your teachers whether what I say is legitimate or not, what I say then is that the whole secret of the sciences and their great predictability is due to *special terminology*. Abolish terminology in any science and you have abolished the science. What I mean, and what I am telling you now is unexpected and new. Thus in the Oxford dictionary you will find good English words which play in life the role of *scientific terminology*, but those terms are not used nor do we know why we should use them.

May I advise my students to watch for a zero in the denominator of your mathematical solution? If it is there the answer is a wrong answer. By chance, perhaps your answer might be right; but do not take chances. So to my students I give advice like that zero in the denominator, and these have to be followed or you will fail. When I tell you a term is a technical term in GS, use it. The term will do the work for you, as it does in mathematics. This is the unexpected. I want to stress this very much. When I tell you a term is technical, use it. Make an effort to use all of them. See the results, and if you do not get results, blame me then, after trial not before. *Evaluation* for all your psycho-logical reactions; it is a *technical term*. You will understand it later when we advance further. Every term you use, see how much of evaluation there is in it. You will see that your feelings are nothing but evaluation. Use the term *evaluation* about anything whenever possible. It is a technical term and is to be used permanently. If you do this you will see the results. Will you remember that when I stress that a term is *technical* in GS, you should use that term. You will find such terms work automatically; unexpectedly as they do in science.

    Now we will proceed. Before going on though, you must translate the terms in everyday use into technical terms. "Love" or "anger", etc., are evaluations. And all this does work, the same way technical terms work in mathematics. When you ask how someone feels you ask how they evaluate something. If you deliberately use the term it very often turns out to be organic evaluation, a smile, the need for food, etc. In terminology the use of terms must be deliberate — how you will translate the use of something into evaluation must be found out. Hunger would be an organic evaluation but in my work I am not so much interested in organic evaluation as in psycho-logical evaluation on the physico-mathematical bases which are in turn based on evaluation. When we have a tested term we deliberately apply that in science. The old terms are unworkable because they do not give us any mechanism. Now evaluation allows scientific evaluation. As a science goes by limitations, as you will see, we are getting away from the broad generalizations by limitations too. Liking or disliking a person is a question of how you evaluate that person. I advise you to work hard on the translation of ordinary English terms into human evaluation. There is a definite formula in GS to be applied and what I say is a general answer to your questions. This formula is, whenever you have a question to ask the other fellow or yourself, the answer always is "I do not know. Let's see." In other words, investigation of facts. See what is what, and what applies to what, and you have your answer. This is scientific. There are a certain amount of important facts that have been neglected. Let me tell you about those facts. Do you suppose you could live without drinking water? You could not live without water; then is not that a part of your environment and in the same manner is not air? Now I will ask you a question that has been neglected. Could you and I live and be human without a linguistic and semantic environment? No? Right.

Is not then a linguistic environment as vital as water and air? Then there is the *meaning*-ful environment; the environment of values. Have you not an environment of values all around you? Can you get away from it? Do you realize then that sanity is a problem of evaluation; that insanity is a problem of misevaluation? Each of you is encircled by a whole environment of values and evaluations. All this is a linguistic and a semantic environment, and the environment of evaluation is as important as air or water. This has been neglected until now.

I advise you to read Carrel's *Man The Unknown*. This is an epoch making book, and he has the authority to rebuke the medical profession who still have sixteenth century standards. What we call medicine, without psychiatry, is only glorified veterinary science. They have disregarded the linguistic and semantic environment. The work of Burridge on colloidal formulations has upset the whole medical theory. His books are published by the Oxford Press and would interest all of you. You may ask me whether my opinion about this work of Burridge is legitimate. You may ask, and you may think it is improper to give such importance to a new work, and I have said that work has exploded all medical theories. You may well ask, "is not that opinion rash?" The answer is very positive. The private theory of Burridge is a very new one; the private colloidal theory of Burridge is of no great importance, it may be wrong because it is so new and it must be tried before it is found correct. But, the constructive revolution is produced because he has taken into account *two* factors, physiological and colloidal. He has *two* mechanisms where the old had only *one*. This taking of the two factors is of importance. Do not become confused that the old facts still remain, but the *interpretations* must be revised.

For example, gravitation as explanation for falling bodies is a foolish answer to a foolish question. Gravitation is an excuse; it explains nothing. But, when

Einstein treats it as a space-time theory the fact remains, but the *interpretations* are different. And when this change is made we are getting closer to mechanisms. They are not worked out yet but there is an inkling of a mechanism here. We are getting closer to facts and mechanisms. The effects have not changed, but the interpretations are different. That is important.

SEMINAR LECTURE TWO

When Einstein started a series of lectures in Berlin he started with a class of two hundred. This was his first lecture. At his second lecture he had ten people and at the third he had five which kept up. I was rather interested whether out of the hundred we had first time if we would have ten tonight and five the next. But I see we have a larger group now than we had before.

I will always sum up what we have accomplished. In the introductory lecture I explained the life necessity for a revision of our orientations by linguistic means, etc. It was necessary to outline what is what; and why are we analysing all this together? For, after all we spend our time here and we ought to know what is the aim before us. Well, in the first lecture I explained to you that the requirements of life are such that they require new orientations; new orientations which the present education is not giving us. Otherwise, we have to introduce new factors in education to prevent and remedy the failure of modern life. I also tried to convey brute facts that affect our modern life. We all are affected by the motorcar, the aeroplane, and the radio. Is your life affected by these? Is your life affected by a question of war and peace? By a question of armaments; by a question of communication? The question of dropping of bombs on you from the aeroplanes? You don't know the 'joy' of it yet, but I do. And we will get more of it probably soon. Will this affect our life? Yes. We must make preparations for it. These preparations affect our taxes too.

I emphasized that whenever electricity is concerned; a magneto in a car, an aeroplane, or a radio; whenever electricity is concerned the old geometries and mechanics will not do at all. They will not work. Otherwise, the actual conditions under which we live depend on non-euclidean and non-newtonian principles. We cannot build up a magneto in a car by euclidean or newtonian methods. It cannot be done. You have mathematicians and physicists here; ask them if what I say is correct. Otherwise, the actual conditions under which we live are no more euclidean and newtonian, but are built up by non-euclidean and non-newtonian disciplines.

I wonder if you see the difference? Euclid and Newton still hold good as far as this house or a bridge, etc., are concerned but only as far as electricity does not enter. Under standard conditions Euclid and Newton may still be just as useful, but not in general. This is the main point. As far as Aristotle is concerned we can arrange a dinner party but we cannot hope for any sort of sanity today if we use aristotelian methods exclusively. Aristotle may provide us with orientation about a dinner table but he will not provide us with orientation concerning our life, which unfortunately is not a dinner table. There are more complex problems in life than fixing a dinner table. In my first lecture, I tried to convey the necessity — not a pleasure, nor a fad — the necessity of a revision of our human orientation as such. I spoke for two hours trying to convey to you the difficulties and the necessities of this revision. Tonight we will begin the course proper.

Before I begin to do this I want to forewarn you that sometimes I am ashamed of lecturing. Yes, ashamed. The reason is that it is all so idiotically simple; yet as President Brewer said, not so easy. Simple but not easy. I want to forewarn you that it has to be taken very seriously if you want to get the benefit. I want to deliver results. I want every person here to get the benefit of it. And knowing the difficulties by experience, I will be going at a very slow pace. I will repeat a great deal to facilitate the training; GS is an empirical natural science and it works when applied. The second 'curse word' I use, I will not tell you the first in public — in private, yes, but in public, no — is "cosmic legislation". Every fool "knows all about the cosmos", but in science we know very little about the cosmos.

I say frankly that if you find any 'cosmic legislation' in my work dismiss the whole thing. You will not find any there. I am talking about facts, facts, facts, and *facts* alone! You can always verify these facts. That is the point. But the moment we agree on a fact stick to it. In mathematical physics when we discover something, say an error in a formula or a disregarded factor in an equation, once discovered it is then corrected, and the old error is abandoned for good. That is mathematical science. We do not do that in life, we live today under great difficulties and we will discover presently vicious factors in human orientations, we will agree because we cannot disagree; yet in life we will not apply what we learn. And that is where we will fail. So here I will not only expound the theory describing facts, old and new facts, but will try to drill you in the application of what we have learned. As you remember in the first lecture we were stressing *predictability*. Have you thought about this by yourselves? What predictability means in life? What predictability does in living? It is a crucial problem; whether predictability in life is important or not. If you could predict that an action or decision would make you unhappy, would you do it? If we could predict some scientific educational problems, should we do what we do in education or should we revise our methods? Then would not predictability be important?

There is private life. How about national and international life? How about England and America nonpredicting that their laxity is encouraging Hitler, world armaments, and another world war? If they could predict would they be so lax? I want the class to be convinced of the extreme importance of predictability. I want educators to understand that if we have predictability of any value — for we may have predictability that is a bluff — this would help us to guide our students toward better adjustment. If we get that, is it not important?

The real problem is predictability. Whether we can get that or not is still a different problem. But should we strive for that predictability? At present mathematics, physics, and mathematical physics are the most predictable sciences there are; and by the study of mathematical physics and their methods we will discover factors of predictability and that is what we are after. Now, I begin to search for factors of predictability.

TERRITORY: S.F.   C.   N.Y.
MAP: C.   S.F.   N.Y.

    The point is predictability. If we compare an actual territory, say San Francisco, Chicago, and New York, with a map which is only a representation of this territory, and put San Francisco in between Chicago and New York, who of you would like to travel by such a map where the cities are in non-corresponding order? What kind of predictability could we have with a map like that? None! Now, the problem is whether we want a predictable map or whether we are willing to accept an unpredictable map. We connect these problems very soon with daily life.

    What could we say about such a map? We could say what we want, but we probably would say that the map is "bad". Would that be true? Yes. We could say that map is "wrong". Would that be true? Could we say that the map is "false"? Etc. Now we are getting down to business. Do any important consequences follow from that kind of statement? We use moral terms, "bad", "wrong", "false", etc., and nothing of importance follows. Do we get any wisdom out of such statements? No. That is the point.

    I advise you to pay attention to linguistic issues. Some terms do not carry important consequences and some terms do. It happens like in mathematical physics some terminology does work, and some verbiage does not. This, what I have said, is a matter of fact. Do not try to understand too much in the beginning because it will confuse you. Take it for granted at present without a full understanding of what is coming. In mathematical sciences which are the best we have, terminology does the work. In life some terminology works and others do not. It is unexpected.

I advise you to make notes very carefully. In the beginning it all is simple; but you will see how, later on when material accumulates, you get confused without notes. It is humanly impossible to take this course without notes. When you listen to what I say, it is very simple; try to apply it. It is very hard. It requires a new orientation, and that is not easy.

We have spoken about the map and the territory. We have used the words "bad", "wrong", and "false", etc., in connection with that map where Chicago is on one side and San Francisco in the middle. You know that with such a map we could not predict the results, etc., of our travel, how could we? I told you that old verbal evaluations of a map like that are unworkable, and we must use expressions about the coordination of that map to that territory and we see that old verbiage did not work. Now we shall see, and what I say here is new, that in the Oxford standard dictionary of the English language we find terms of standard language which play the role of scientific terminology, which work like physico-mathematical terminology. We find that if we abolish the terminology of a science we have abolished the science. And yet we find in life words that play the role of scientific terminology. That is unexpected. It just happened; such terms exist except we never use those terms. We have them but we never use them. The main difference between GS and the old system is that we introduce those new terms and use them. Later on you will understand why they are so important — they work like scientific terms work in science. And, there is no escape from it. Use those terms and you will see the results. Nothing but application will do.

You remember the other night I stressed the term *evaluation*? I suggested that you apply the term evaluation whenever you can. Later on you will see why it is so important. The term alone will do the work, will sharpen your intelligence, your acuteness, and your capacities; yes, just the use of that term *evaluation*. As the other fellow may not understand you let him go his way, but use the term for yourselves, and then you can translate your consequences later into his language. But, use the term evaluation to get the results and you can translate it later. Use these terms for yourself and how you translate them for the other fellow makes no difference. The new orientation comes with the use of those terms.

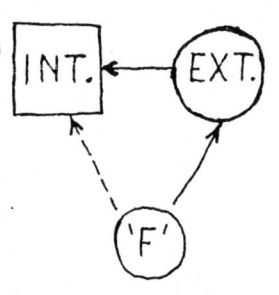

If you use the new terms for yourself, then the new terminology can always be translated later for somebody else; but then you will appear as a 'genius' for something new will appear in your analysis. If you take any set of 'facts' ('F') and you analyse them in the old intensional (INT) way, you will get some sort of result, but if you analyse them in the new way which I call extensionalization (EXT), you will get some new results; but then you can always translate them into the old way. But you will get new results, and you will appear so intelligent and very gifted. Why? Because you make this new extensional analysis for yourself. You cannot follow this completely or fully understand it at this stage but you will understand all that later. I am not only lecturing on that new method, but I am drilling you in it.

Remember that my whole presentation is already extensional. It is already an exhibition of what is going to come theoretically. And if you will follow the new method you will have the best possible analysis of life situations at a date and even scientific researches are facilitated. That is toward what we will be working. You realize, possibly, the situation in connection with the territory-map. That the map is incorrect; the map should correspond to the territory. Under such conditions of the map as it stands could we have *maximum probability* of *predictability*? These words sound similar but do not mix them. They are different. Maximum probability of predictability is our main problem.

I have explained to you already that when we use the terms *good*, *bad*, etc. that these terms are unworkable. When we say the map is "good", "bad", "wrong", etc., which happen to be true, did those words carry us somewhere, give important results, even though they happen to be true? No. Here again I introduce technical terms, and when I say "technical terms", remember I mean terms you have to use yourself permanently. New technical terms should never be abandoned, and we never abandon them in science.

For maximum usefulness a map should be *similar in structure* to the territory. I suppose the words "similarity of structure" convey something to you in the ordinary sense. The main point here is then, that similarity of structure is our most important point of mathematical physics and in mathematics, in spite of the fact that you may understand it in the ordinary sense. Similarity of the physical and symbolic relations. Is our map similar in structure with the territory? On such a map is predictability possible? I am not overburdening you with the technical side of the problem. It is very complex. But the ordinary meaning of the words that a map should be similar in structure to the territory, should convey something to you. This is a very important point.

Now how shall we define similarity of structure? I will speak to you only in terms of common sense. It is to be defined in terms of *order*, in the sense of *betweenness*. You understand this term betweenness? If not consult the Oxford dictionary.

I always speak to a seminar class seriously, but don't be shy about laughing. Later on we will find another thing, that a great many of our human troubles are only artificial verbal bubbles, and when they are pricked they burst so there is nothing left but to laugh; so by the end of the seminars we will be laughing quite a bit because nine-tenths of our troubles are verbal bubbles.

We define the term *similarity of structure* in terms of order, and order in terms of betweenness. The term *order* is of fundamental importance — because mathematical physics can be represented in terms of multi-dimensional order. You do not need at present to understand this term "multi-dimensional". I merely said what I did for your information that mathematical physics can be represented in terms of multi-dimensional order. Otherwise, if we apply the term *order* to human affairs we have a common term which bridges human affairs with exact sciences.

Of late, Professor Kurt Lewin has applied extensional mathematical topological methods to 'psychology' with very far reaching results. This is proof that mathematical methods, strictly mathematical, can be applied to 'psychology'. You should read this book of Lewin's, *Principles of Topological Psychology* (McGraw-Hill, N. Y.). Topology is the most general 'science of space'. Not 'space' in the restricted sense, as you know it, but 'space' in a general way. I want to stretch your imagination a little, it will do no harm. I would like you to answer a general question: What is your "space of life"? Your life? Does the "space" of any of your lives include your staff of professors and your colleagues? Do they enter into the "space of your life", the environment of your life? Don't you see the way things widen up? Doesn't the water you drink affect your organism? The fact is that we have here iron in the water. The point is whether it enters your "space of life". Does your staff here enter into your "space of life"? The span of your life? Do you see to what extent we are enlarging the notion of "space", taking it as environment including all available factors?

That is where topology comes in. Topology is based on the relation of the inclusion of the part in the whole. You can see how every one of us, and how every major concern of ours, includes the inclusion of the part in the whole. Each part of you, for instance your own private life, you are part of a community and a country, subjected to conditions in each, outside the college life in general. Otherwise, your private life is a part of a whole, a part of a whole of a whole. That is, the strictly mathematical foundations of topology represent analogous issues. And the topological 'psychology' you get becomes very general because mathematical methods are very general. This method can be applied to each of our lives, even though it is very general. Thus 'psychology' can be based on mathematical equations and bases. Unfortunately very few psychiatrists know anything about mathematics, and very few mathematicians know anything about 'psychology'.

Newspapers can use this method too. They should be socialized. They should become interested in social orientations, and not just plain news. They should become an educational factor. Scripps of Scripps-Howard newspapers was a very fine man and he founded Science Service with this very aim. But through all his work, he could not understand the role of money in life. He died with the question of "what is money"? Money is only a symbol for human agreement. Can I eat it if you don't want to take it? What can I do with it if you don't want to take it? It is only a symbol.

Well, going back to our situation of the territorial map. Did we agree that the maximum probability of predictability of a map is due to similarity of structure between the map and the territory based on order? Was that clear? We enlarged that problem to the point that through multi-dimensional order we will have mathematical physics. Otherwise introducing the mathematical term *order* into ordinary human affairs, we are linking mathematical sciences to human affairs. Nothing much is accomplished yet but it is a common term, and further advance is made possible. It is only a question now of dimensionality. You do not need to fully understand that because there is no reason to go further into that. That is number one. Number two, the term *order* has connection with ordering of reaction — you will understand this later; it is the main point of GS — through the term order we physically stimulate the human cortex. This is one of the greatest points of GS. You will hear a lot about it later. This was not expected; it just happened. And it works that way. Otherwise, we are getting *physical* means to stimulate our cortex through *ordering of reactions*. You will understand this better later on. Do you see the connections? Will you agree that all we have done so far appears in a way idiotically simple? Are you not surprised that only in the twentieth century do we begin to speak about such subjects? Don't you see the simplicity of it? Pathetic! It is not a slur. Similarity of structure is extremely simple and yet no one paid any attention to it until GS. *For maximum probability of maximum predictability we must have a map similar in structure to the territory.*

Now, let us see what can be said further on that subject. Observation suggests three simple premises which are very far reaching. On those three premises we either agree or disagree for this is the only point where we can quarrel.

PREMISES:
1. Map *is not* territory
2. Map is *not all* of the territory
3. Map is *self-reflexive*

1. *Map is not territory.* Any dissenting in this group? Who does not agree? Do you all agree? Do you

all accept this, that the *map is not* the territory? Are you fully convinced of this? It will take us the rest of the seminars to show you what I will say now. So I will make a statement which I am unable to back up at this date. In every field, personal, human, national, etc., 'insanity' included, old orientations involved an *is* of 'identity'. It will take many hours to make it clear to you and remember that we as a group have *denied* flatly that *is* of identity: *Map is not the territory*. If it can be shown that the old is based on the 'is' of identity, we can see where the old stands.

2. *Map not all of territory*. Did you ever see a map that would cover "all of the territory"? No. So we make another second premise that the map does *not* cover 'all' of the territory. Most of the old orientations are based on 'all' which we flatly deny. We deny the 'allness' as a group. When we deny this unlimited 'all' we are beginning to get at the bottom of the difficulty. Suppose I am a president of a college and I make statements for the group for 'all times' to come. Am I not a dogmatist? I make statements, correct perhaps for today, but not correct for *all times to come*. If your statement is *limited* to the date can you be an absolutist? Can you see what happens by comparing the old and the new evaluations? That is the second premise.

3. *Map is self-reflexive.* Imagine that I would make on this table here a 'perfect' map of Olivet College. Would this lecturer here be in the map? Would this lecture hall be in the map? Would the map of the map be there? That is self-reflexiveness. When you have the map of the map you have a self-reflexiveness of the map. Now that characteristic goes on ad infini-

tum. For this has no limits any more. That characteristic is called self-reflexiveness, as yet it has been completely neglected. Self-reflexiveness has been known about maps for some years; it was discovered by Professor Royce of Harvard, but was then neglected.

I want to call your attention to a fundamental issue that those three premises are the first that have ever been written that contrast the old with the new, which are the foundations of GS. The first new premise: "*map is not territory*" while the old is based on 'is' of identity which we completely deny. The second premise "map is not all of territory", while the old was based on 'all' which we flatly deny. And the question of self-reflexiveness has been entirely neglected. At the bottom of every difficulty you will find the old premises which we flatly deny. We as a group do this, and the old has to accept. In the first two premises we are bringing about a complete denial. And the third premise has been entirely neglected. In fact this self-reflexiveness has ruined the foundation of mathematics until this day.

I was speaking about map-territory interrelationship. This applies to every form of representation; among others, language. That is where the important problems come in. I started with maps but the issues are concerned with something deeper than maps. Can you see my walking stick? Do you have a picture of it in your brain? Can you lend me your brain for me to walk with? Is your *representation* then of the stick a *map* or is it the stick itself? It is only a map. Well that is where the importance comes in. The *picture* of the stick *is not* the stick. Later on this will become very complex. So when we speak about those three premises, try to apply them to your orientations in life. The word *is not* the fact, the situation or what not. The word does *not* cover *all* the characteristics of an object or of a situation. I want you to digest and absorb the three premises, for they are the foundations of GS. And obviously language is *self-reflexive* in the sense that in language we can speak about language, and every kind of difficulty may happen if we don't know about self-reflexiveness and are not conscious of it. In language we can speak *about* language but if we don't know it difficulties will happen. This fact has produced the difficulties in mathematical foundations which even until today are not solved. These difficulties have originated in self-reflexiveness of language.

I have to refer to speaking as compared with making noises. I called some manners of speaking after Stanley Hall, "masturbation of the salivary glands". Well, we do a lot of this masturbation — verbalizations that are meaningless. I wonder if you are getting the importance of this. If I would ask you in English whether blah blah is tra tra or not; would that be asking a question? No. I would just make a noise; say nothing and ask nothing although I could have spelled it and put a question mark after it. Would that question mark be a question? Do you realize that at the bottom of most of our 'philosophies' there is a great deal of noise? To close I will emphasize the importance of discriminating between words which symbolize something and noises which symbolize nothing.

SEMINAR LECTURE THREE

There is a standard neurotic mechanism, a sick mechanism, which by now affects the whole world as a result of the war; namely, the difficulty in articulation. This is very difficult and to my students I give this advice: clear up your language, clear that up as a physical symptom. Learn to pronounce your words clearly. It is a physical symptom. The old world is ailing and with the clarification of articulation, you will see that things will happen in your brain. These issues happen together.

As always, I start my seminar with a summary of what we have accomplished. We have compared a territory with a map. That comparison was so important because all our representations and verbal issues are only maps which are not the territory or the 'facts'. You will see later how far that simple analysis goes. At present it seems to you perhaps trivial. Later on you will see to what extent it is not trivial. When it comes to an actual table, is that speakable? No. That is an old story and what you say *about* a table; *is it* the table? No. Now, as far as the table is concerned, it sounds simple. How about your life and your loves and hates, etc. — all your feelings? Do you realize you *identify* them with your verbal issues; that your verbalizations are not really it? Pinch your finger. Is that what you directly feel? Don't you realize that that actual feeling *is not* verbalization? It is on an *unspeakable* level. You must pinch your finger before you can be convinced that it is not the same as what you say about it. Here we apply the first premise, "*is not*".

One of the main problems which we deal with in GS is in the discrimination or non-identification between the word and the objective levels. It is fundamental that we start with a *discrimination* between what we directly *feel* and what you *say* because what you feel *is not* what you say. And this is where we identify our verbal issues with feelings. We mix or identify in internal evaluation those two entirely different issues. We must try to fight against it.

So we have compared the territory with the map and we have concluded that for the *maximum predictability*, for the *maximum probability* of *predictability*, we have to have a form of representation — which is *similar in structure* in terms of order. I have to forewarn you that in science where we have the maximum of predictability we go by this similarity of structure between a theory and facts. Let us not hide behind words. Let's have a look at facts; what we call a 'scientific theory' represents a language of special structure, based on terminology. Otherwise, terminology involves structural assumptions which are structurally *implied* in the terminology. Otherwise, what we call a theory is really nothing but a language of special structure.

The few structural terms do that. They introduce a language of *special structure*. That is all a 'theory' amounts to. A few terms do that. So, let's not hide behind verbalistic walls like 'theory'. *Every theory* is based on *terminology*; and the *terminology* involves special kinds of structural assumptions which are sometimes true and sometimes false. Let us not talk about 'theory' alone. Every theory involves a *language* of *special structure*. I will give you an example which you will understand better. When Einstein is speaking about space-time, say, and we are explaining that to laymen; do you know what is the usual remark? "Oh, what you mean is 'space' and 'time'." Do you know that that translation has eliminated Einstein's whole work? But, what we mean is the hyphen, space-time being indivisible; and if you say "space *and* time" you will have broken down Einstein's whole theory. Why? Because the whole thing is of different structure. The latter is a language of different structure. The first (space-time) is the language of four-dimensional structure, while the second is a language of three plus one structure. Are you willing to admit that when you add three plus one and make it four you have gone one step further? If you have three plus one dimension and you finish the job, say four dimensions, have you made a step forward or not? Is it difficult? You are witnessing steps in civilization, in cultural advance, when three plus one equals four. Take it very simply to begin with. Have no difficulties about dimensionality. There is nothing mystic about it.

Dimensionality implies a number of factors. The number we need to know before we know something. Motion involves four dimensions. Otherwise, 'space' and 'time' are indivisibly connected. Look at the smoke of my cigarette. You see what is going on. How many factors — just fancy, for we can do no better — do you have to know to follow up what is going on in this smoke. At least four? No, a million would not cover it. I am trying to convey that question of dimensionality over to you. Following that smoke how many factors do you need to know, to get hold of that cloud of smoke? Otherwise, that cloud of smoke is million-dimensional. Can we separate 'space' and 'time'? No. If you can do it — which is impossible — in the older verbalistic way we could separate 'space' and 'time'; in the new we do not because we stick to realities.

To return to our discussion, we were talking about our three fundamental premises. (1) Map is not territory; (2) Map is not all of territory; (3) Map is self-reflexive. We have shown in the last seminar that what was said about map-territory applies to words and facts. For maximum probability of predictability we need to have a similarity of structure between language and the facts. Investigate, find out whether our language is similar in structure to the facts or not. If our language would be similar in structure like we have in mathematical physics would we have the maximum predictability? Yes. If it is not similar would we have the maximum predictability? No.

Is that not our important problem for investigation? Investigate the facts for that similarity of structure which exists or does not exist. It is important whether the language is similar in structure or not.

We know facts as we know them. Now the question is whether our habitual language is similar in structure to the facts or not. That is a problem of fact. Can we find that by speculation? No, we have to find that out by inspection of known facts. What would happen if our language would not be similar in structure to the facts?

Would we have predictability? Don't you see the price we pay; and what would happen if we adjust the structure of language to the structure of facts? Would predictability appear? I want you to realize how crucial a problem for investigation this is. To a certain extent that whole issue is dramatic. Let me give you an example on which all of science and all of the white civilization depends. If you have a physical chain made up of links which happen to be structurally a *serial* structure, now we use a language of serial structure, a, b, c, d, e, f, etc.; 1, 2, 3, 4, 5, 6, etc. The physical structure is serial and our language is serial. The question then is whether they are similar in structure or not. Serial structure and a serial language — yes, they are similar.

```
 ◯ ◯ ◯ ◯ ◯ ◯
 1   2   3   4   5   6   etc.
 a   b   c   d   e   f   etc.
```

And, now I will show you miracles of science and civilization, all of it based on similarity of structure and predictability. We do not know the facts, yet in life we are after facts. We are after them; we are after predictability. Now look at the miracle we can produce in predictability. I am not supposed to know facts, and will use mere verbal speculations, but look what happens. I predict two is between one and three. Do you agree with that *verbal* predictability? Let us verify that and we find in fact that in the physical chain link 2 is between 1 and 3. If we have a language of similar structure, you can predict the physical facts. That is the strength and foundation of all science. Do you realize the psychiatric value of that and the sanity value of it? But, let me tell you one thing, if you had predictability somewhat in all things, with predictability we have expectation verified which saves us from shocks and so constitutes factors of sanity.

Do you know what happened in the war? Soldiers who expected horrors got them but had no nervous breakdowns. But those soldiers that did not expect them did break down quite often. Predictability! Otherwise, expectation. If you expect horrors and you get them they won't harm you nervously. But if you do not expect them they may harm you nervously. The shock does the harm. Take those facts as facts.

I spoke on the basis of endless data. Now one of the greatest benefits of science is predictability. Elimination of shocks because we expect them — predictability. I want you to understand how everything ties up with everything else. And the scientific predictability based on similarity of structure between representation and the facts, and sanity and adjustments to the facts, and maladjustment based on shocks; I want you to understand how they all come together.

Now we have to investigate a matter of fact. We will investigate whether our language is similar in structure to the known facts or not. This is a very common sense investigation. It will be a shock, and I want you to live up to the shock. As a matter of fact you will want to do this at first, but you will not, unless you work very hard. Now, we will investigate whether our language is similar in structure or not to the facts. It is an important investigation which will help predictability in our life. If it is similar in structure then maximum predictability is possible. Here I introduce you to something that is new. Namely, an empirical investigation of a new type of

Lecture Three 39

facts which are linguistic and semantic. Facts which are just as much facts as this box. But this is a new line of inquiry: namely, linguistic and semantic facts. The facts are simple; the novelty is that we never thought of investigating the similarity of structure of a language with the facts.

Can we actually divide 'matter', 'space', and 'time', here? (Showing a pencil.) In 'mental' hospitals and chairs of 'philosophy' they try to do it. If you could divide 'matter', 'space', and 'time'; if you could take away 'matter' from this cane, would there be a cane? If you take 'space' ('space' in quotation marks mind you) away it will be a mathematical point but no cane. If you take away 'time' there would be a flash but again no cane. This applies to you, and to everything else you know. This to be this, you to be you, house to be house, food to be food, anything else involves indivisible 'matter', 'space', and 'time' which are only linguistic categories which in nature are indivisible. Do you understand the facts of nature as explained? That is the structure and the facts of nature, that 'matter' 'space' and 'time' cannot be divided.

Now, how about verbal and linguistic issues? Can you *verbally* divide 'matter', 'space', and 'time'? Yes. Now here comes a question. Is a language which *can divide* what cannot be divided physically, similar in structure? Obviously not. If you have a language not similar in structure to the facts, we can not expect maximum predictability, and must change the structure of language. A map where we had San Francisco between Chicago and New York is misguiding and sometimes dangerous, and such maps should not be used. That is what we have to do with the language of old structure. There is no other way out. This is a sharp issue too. If we say quit the language, the next question would be whether we have to hang ourselves or not. No, the moment we realize that a certain problem exists we always solve it. Remember that. So instead of hanging ourselves we page Einstein who has established a non-elementalistic language of space-time where 'space' and 'time' are not divided and so-called 'matter' enters in a form of curvature of space-time.

I want to introduce to you, and as most of you will take some sort of professional career, I want to suggest some terms as crucial. One of them is that the facts of nature are *non-elementalistic*. Otherwise, the factors of our so-called elements cannot be separated. They are *non-elementalistic*. Otherwise, the facts of nature are *not split up*, otherwise they are non-elementalistic. Now our languages, the old ones, give us forms of representation which are elementalistic. This is advice to you to pay particular attention to elementalism and non-elementalism. If we make an elementalistic analysis we will find it is not satisfactory because the 'facts' are *non-elementalistic*. And you could not make the language fit. Now are you beginning to see the sharpness of this issue? We established that such a language is not similar in structure to the facts where 'space' and 'time' cannot be split.

Now let us go to a situation which is closer to us. Can you divide, split, actual 'body-mind'? If you are split you are a corpse, not a *living being*. Can you split any living being? If you say you can, you are a dementia praecox in an asylum. So actually we cannot split body-mind. Can you split *actually* 'emotion' and 'intellect'? Now remember you are hanging yourself if you admit you cannot split them, yet the next minute you will split them in life because you use elementalistic orientations and language. In life you admit anything, but will not apply it. In GS if we admit anything we stick to it. We cannot split 'body-mind' in actuality. We cannot split 'intellect' and 'emotion' yet we can split them verbally.

Such a language is not similar in structure to the facts. What shall we do? Quit! But the question remains whether we shall hang ourselves in addition or not. Just to say "quit" sounds simple, sounds easy — yes, just quit and what? The *what* of quitting is an important problem. It is simple to quit but then what? It is not so simple. The answer is page GS. Here we do *not* split verbally what cannot be split actually. You will use the term "semantic reaction" instead of 'thought' or 'emotions'. We have *semantic reactions* which are of a totalistic non-elementalistic sort of form like space-time, where 'emotions' and 'intellect' are not split; *evaluation* which borders on mathematical physics which involves 'emotion' and 'intellect'. When you evaluate, you respond non-elementalistically and the term 'evaluation' is non-elementalistic because it involves 'emotion' and 'intellect'. When you *evaluate*, will this term apply to your 'feelings'? Yes. Let's look at the old language of emotion. Would that mean a sort of *evaluation*? "Emotion" and "intellect" are elementalistic terms, unfit for communication, and you have to use them with quotation marks for warning. Is that clear, that the old way of orientation and language where we split verbally what we cannot split actually, is *not similar in structure* with the facts? Otherwise, misleading, misguiding? That is why we are getting more and more maladjusted, because we are getting misguided by a map that is not similar in structure to the facts. I want you to get that and particularly because you are partly scientifically inclined.

Everything we know will have to be revised. For to begin with, one of the very serious dangers is the use of elementalistic terms where the facts are non-elementalistic. Take your own life, of that life I will not go into the details, but you work at it. Will you describe yourself; each of you just sitting here on those chairs listening to lectures; describe yourself as much as you wish, in as many details as you care to. Do you ever cover 'all' the details of your inheritance, your protoplasm, experiences of childhood and what not? Do you make any description of yourself which covers 'all' the facts of yourselves? Don't you see that life is non-elementalistic, but your language is elementalistic? Can you describe yourself with 'all' characteristics? It cannot be done. Otherwise, you must be aware of the importance of our premises.

You know how rapidly you build up your conviction, that that 'is' that. Don't you know that you will have to take into consideration 'all' characteristics? Is that humanly possible? No! And yet you *act* as if you had taken into consideration 'all' characteristics. Don't you see the danger of it? I want you to understand from a private life point of view whether you humanly can take into consideration 'all' characteristics, 'all' factors which have made each of you what you are. Otherwise, for some sane orientation should we be aware of the "*not all*"? If we have the old fashioned orientations, life goes in the old unhappy way. Can you have a sane judgment? If you would preserve the old fashioned orientations of 'allness', which is unattainable humanly, can you have a sound orientation? Otherwise, we have to be trained in a new discipline, in a new order. Otherwise, you will make your decisions in a *hypothetical* sense, just as we do in science. We take statistical information and make hypothetical judgments. Let us *know* they are *hypothetical judgments*.

The question I will ask the class is quite simple. It is not a tricky question. The answer will be important. Now, outside of the hard seats, are you quite comfortable here? Are you more or less quite happy here tonight? What I will stress now is a fundamental issue which all of you neglect. Assuming then that all of you are quite happy here, do you realize that this is tragic, that all of your so-called 'happiness' here is based on blind faith or assumptions, which are unconscious? Blind faith in the architect of the building and the management of the school, that the floor will not go through. Don't you see the blind faith of it? In science we call that *assumptions*. Did it ever occur to you how much blind faith you live upon? The whole of your life is based on blind faith. Remember this is the factor of so-called human knowledge. All of it, namely *necessary assumptions*, are at the bottom of it and what I call blind faith is called assumption. Only in geometry in the old did we begin to deal fundamentally with investigation of the assumption. Very few mathematicians know that fundamental postulates (assumptions) are based on blind faith. Let us call a spade a spade. Namely, a postulate, which is the most polite way of saying it is nothing but an assumption; and in a still less polite way, blind faith.

We have made today an investigation of a postulate — I will use postulate and assumption indifferently, but anyway it will mean blind faith. Very few mathematicians know that mere investigation of postulates, and I mean assumptions or blind faith, is not enough. In the beginning, years ago, there was the belief that investigation, verification of postulates, was enough. It turned out not to be enough. You have to follow up the theorems that follow from the postulates, until they verify the postulates. Otherwise, the theory has to be developed to a full extent following from postulates, to theory, and then the theory has to be tested to verify the postulates. Remember the three premises. Never forget them. They are the key to the whole problem.

These premises are the departure from the old orientation which is unfit for us in 1937, because it is *not similar* in structure to the facts of life. Do you understand the difference between elementalistic and non-elementalistic orientations? If you do, then I shall go on.

As usual let us go back to our premises; 'not all', otherwise what I said about the structure of language is still 'not all'. We will make another investigation and this is the one of the key problem to the whole issue. What I will do is very serious although you may laugh if you care to. But what I do is not really laughable. Here is an Olivet world. I am a stranger. I see some bubbles of protoplasm before me. I begin to investigate. I investigate that fellow, and that fellow and that fellow, and what do I find out? This is very difficult. Do you know what I discover? And, you will discover it too. I find that that fellow here is an absolute individual in the world. There is no other 'identical' to him here. This applies to the rest of us. And it applies to everything you know. Literally everything you know. A box of matches lies here on the desk. Are any two matches in that box 'identical'? We are discovering then a neglected yet fundamental law of nature; namely, the *law of non-identity*. Never forget that. It is contained in the second premise, *is not all*. It is a complete denial of identity. Identity, being defined as absolute sameness in all characteristics, is non-existent. We have discovered a fundamental natural law of this world, the law of non-identity. Do you realize that this natural law of non-identity is universal? It is a matter of fact. It is empirical.

In four dimensions any particle at any moment (different) cannot be identical with itself. I was asked by a mathematician whether an object is identical with itself, and I answered that he must not be familiar with modern mathematics and physics. I knew he was teaching them. I asked him then if he had ever heard of mathematical physics? He said, "Why I am teaching that too." Then I told him I would *deny* that any *electronic process* is ever 'identical' with itself. Are you 'identical' with yourself from second to second? What you know about yourself should tell you that you are not 'identical' with yourself from moment to moment. Do you realize the shame, the pity, that that kind of analysis should be taken up in the twentieth century, because it seems so simple and so strange to us. Do you see that this should be the basis for education? And yet the educational system outside of very few forward looking schools, and in parts only, completely neglects this problem in education. That kind of answer as a proof of orientations about 'identity' is common generally, but I will quote another instance closer to our premise. Non-identity is the premise but it is non-identity in 'all' characteristics. Identity is defined as absolute sameness in *all* characteristics. You may be similar, you may have a nose and may have a mouth and some teeth even, but you are not identical to another person because '*not all*' characteristics of you are 'identical' to the other. If you have only one characteristic similar, do you have 'identity'? When we approach the limits of classification in science the characteristics of *one* molecule differ from the general characteristics of groups of molecules and atoms. Those are matters of facts in general science.

The same is true among ourselves. That 'psychology' of each one of us taken separately is different than when we are in a group, herd 'psychology' or group 'psychology' is different than individual 'psychology'. Non-elementalistic orientations, non-detachment from the environment, from the group, from the environment of which we are all victims; non-detachment from semantic environment from which we cannot escape; we are born into some system of evaluation. Can you be separated from that system, whatever it was? Otherwise, the non-elementalistic character of the *semantic* or *linguistic environment*. Does that leave us in a situation where some of the most vital factors of our life are neglected? Why do we fool about the analysis of water? Why do we fool about the 'water environment' and the 'air environment', and entirely disregard the *linguistic* and *semantic environment*? In GS we investigate those factors which have before been neglected. I am always taking a sort of physico-mathematical as well as psychiatric attitude towards our problems because we have so long neglected them. In our *human orientation* they were neglected.

Now, taking into consideration these factors as important factors, later I will explain them more fully, you will see the terrific consequences of this neglect. I might just tell you now about this in advance. Do you all understand the English word, "incest"? Sexual intercourse within the family. Well, take the *semantic environment*; I can give no better example than that. In white civilization as a matter of statistics we do not survive incest, never mind why. Wherever we have incest, even not physical but perhaps symbolic incest, we do not survive it. It always ends in prostitution, criminality, or 'mental' illness. In Egypt in the old days of the Pharaohs, incest among them was the rule and did not do any harm. Not any harm at all. Why? Semantic environment. They had a theory that incest was not harmful. Otherwise, evaluation, semantic environment; and the fact that brother was married to sister, etc., did not matter. What did not do harm in their society, in their semantic environment, is not survived in ours. You see that I speak facts. Do you begin to see what *semantic environment* means? Evaluational environment. Is that getting clear? That the physical facts often do not matter in comparison with semantic facts.

Incest as a matter of statistics in our society, slums or no slums, we never survive incest. If we have this we have either prostitution, criminality, or 'insanity'. Now, physically the facts remain, physically you and I and the rest of us differ little from the Egyptian. Among them incest was the evaluational rule, and no harm was done. We do not survive it. What do you suppose the factors are, physical or semantic? That is all I wanted to ask you. All I wanted to show you, that the physical facts often *matter less* than the semantic factors of evaluation. In one society the same semantic factor will play a different role than in another. One primitive may have a simple disease but goes to a white hospital and dies; and a primitive who would die under white control goes to his primitive medicine man and is 'cured'. Problems of evaluation are, as often as not, more important than problems of physical factors. Physical facts the same, but semantic factors different. Novelty, shock, evaluation account for many of the deaths in the wars. Is that clear? Some of you may already have had what is called 'sex troubles', 'sex difficulties'.

You don't know to what extent it is tragically true that your 'sex difficulties' and 'troubles' are often not due and are not connected with the sex organs. Often have nothing to do with them. All in the head. Clear up this mess and your other difficulties will clear up. What we talk about as 'sex glands' today has little to do with the 'sex organs'. There are few people in the world that are physically defective, but many are semantically defective. You are beginning to see how semantic problems play a great part in life? Problems in *evaluation*, pure and simple. Clear up the troubles in your evaluations and the rest will clear up too. I am trying to convey the fact that *semantic environment* is so important because we cannot escape from some semantic environment. Did I convince you that this semantic environment is as important as your physical environment? Incest we cannot survive while the Egyptian did. The physical facts are the same but the difficulty was in the semantic environment, and the problems are of *evaluation*. You understand that the problems of evaluation, which are inside your brains, I call them semantic factors, play such an extremely important role which until now has been entirely neglected? Any questions? This applies to every field of human endeavor. Can you fancy being free and remaining human, and still be free from semantic environment? ... Well, let's stop here for tonight. Good night.

SEMINAR LECTURE FOUR

As usual I will start with a short summary of what we have accomplished. The lecture tonight in spite of its simplicity will be particularly difficult and I will speak very slowly for I want you to understand what I am saying. When we come to historical departures from the old, those departures are rather difficult to absorb. You remember, that when Einstein started his work there was a general opinion that only twelve people in the world understood Einstein? Now this is not true and it was never true. It merely took a new generation to absorb Einstein. Today every young university student in physics is an einsteinist. Before we are through with these seminars you will also be einsteinists but it took a new generation to make einsteinists out of students.

I am glad to see that there are very few old people here, for they are often hopeless. You will see later why. It is a matter of colloids, of chemistry, which cannot be avoided, that a person cannot remain young. And this is why science goes so slowly. We are ruled still by the older generation and it is out of the question that the older generation should understand the new generation. What I will explain tonight is not only of fundamental importance for GS, but it is a sharp break with the old in which even you, as young people, are trained. You, as young people, are trained in the old, and this departure is categorical. In mathematics and physics when we discover an error in the old we abandon the old. That is what we do in science. You will have great difficulty in abandoning the old because in the nursery the old has been forced upon you and we mostly are doomed to live steadily in the old orientation. You have all lived steadily in the old orientation.

Today I will bring to you a proof and an example where the old is incorrect. If we are scientific at all as we should be, then there is nothing left to do but disregard and discard the old, which you will see for yourself is totally insufficient. Evaluate the old, establish something new, and then accept and utilize that new. That is what we must do. Lip service to the new is not good enough. We have to establish errors in the old, revise them, then through revision, establish something new that is more compatible with the facts of life as we know them, not yesterday, but today. And having established that, we must apply it. That application is most difficult. I make this preface simply to draw your attention to the fact that although all I have to say is idiotically simple yet it is extremely difficult. It would take us six months of steady lectures every day before I could show you to a full extent this application of those new orientations.

This is an analysis of facts, whatever *facts* are; and then, having analyzed the facts we establish *principles* out of those facts. And, they have to be commonsense and ordinary wisdom. I want you to agree on that. I want your agreement so that you will 'hang' yourself, if you agree with everything I tell you here. Why don't you stick to it then? In science we stick to it but in life we do

Lecture Four

not. We do lip service, but we do not stick to it. I will repeat what we have covered so far.

We have covered the territory-map. We take a map in which the towns are in the wrong order. Now such a map is not fit to travel by. We do not have predictability for traveling by such a map. Then such a map is harmful. We have analyzed different kinds of languages and what could we say about the map like that? We have said it is "bad", "wrong", and "*whatnot*". I told you that language would not work and you agreed with that. It led us nowhere. *Moral terms*, but they do not give us any consequences. Then we use a language of new structure out of which consequences follow. From the language "good", "bad", etc., nothing followed. But we have established a new language that becomes already technical terminology, in which we have said, for maximum usefulness, the map must be *similar in structure* to the territory. And we have defined similarity of structure in terms of *order*. Namely, that for the similarity of structure the territory must be in the same order as the map. Namely, similarity of structure can be expanded further to *multi-dimensional order* which covers all mathematical physics. Otherwise, the term 'order' in many dimensions is a workable term and a term which bridges human affairs with mathematical physics, and science. That is the power of a common term which links science and life. We know this can be done and we are going ahead with it. That similarity of structure is necessary for predictability and predictability is a factor for our happiness. After this seminar, think it over for yourself. Fancy what predictability, if it were possible, would mean to your life.

You have probably heard all about the great tragedy of the World War [1914-1918]. You know something about Hitler and the mad armaments — for which you will pay. All that is a question of predictability. If the Kaiser had known England and America would join in the Great War, there would have been no war. If the League of Nations, sincerely supported by England and United States, would agree that there should be no Hitler, there would be no Hitler. No one wants to commit suicide. It is a question of predictability. Why then do we have a Hitler and armaments? Because England and America did not say verbally "stop it". It is a question of *predictability*. We can predict that under certain conditions if 'so and so' happens, 'so and so' will happen, but we have to be clear in our power of formulation and express clearly in our heads what was clear in our language. Then things would, or would not, happen. I am driving here a very important point in connection with predictability. That, if we are clear in our heads and clear in our speaking and we know what we are driving at, things become simpler. Is that clear? I ask you to investigate the problem of the bearing of predictability on your daily private, national, and international life. This is a subject matter for you to think about. The more you get secure in these issues the more progress for you there. We have discovered that similarity of structure between the map-territory is the fundamental issue for predictability. Predictability is absolutely fundamental. Predictability depends on the similarity of structure between the map-language and the territory-fact. I have shown that to you before, but I will repeat: The whole power of science and the whole of civilization is based on predictability and similarity of structure. For example, I have here a physical chain made of links which happens to be a serial structure. We use a *serial language*, like 1, 2, 3, 4, and 5. Both are serial then. The chain is serial and the language is serial; they are both similar in structure then. We should expect to predict then. I will predict then. Not looking at the facts, I will predict that the third link is between the second and fourth. Otherwise I have predicted facts, and those facts happen. This is so simple, but it is a far-reaching principle. The whole of civilization and the whole of science depends on this principle. If you wish, sanity itself depends on that predictability. Why? For the simple reason that a great deal of 'mental' illness is built up by shocks and fear due to uncertainty and unpredictability. A good many 'mental' maladjustments would be eliminated if we could predict 'something' would happen, and 'something' happened. If we have predictability, we have no shock. Imagine that we predict that this floor will fall through and it does, and we fall through with it. We may break our necks, but we do not become nervous wrecks because we would have expected it. We had a good deal of proof of this in the war. Because you do not expect horrors, you break down when those horrors occur. Those who expect horrors do not break down. And those soldiers who were actually wounded were so busy about their wounds that they did not even break down.

Then we have established three premises which follow the analysis of the situation. We have established three new premises, contradicting the old premises which, by the way, have never been set down. We have lived by them for thousands of years but they have never been compiled. We have established here the new and they are:

1) That the map *is not* the territory,
2) That the map does not cover all the characteristics of the territory; *not all*, and
3) That the map is self-reflexive.

I want you thoroughly to understand that self-reflexiveness. We start with the map. An ideal map, say, of Olivet would include this house. It would include me making the map. Otherwise, in an ideal map with 'all' characteristics, which is really impossible, you would have the map of the map, of the map, *endlessly*. That is called *self-reflexiveness*. You cannot realize the tragedy of that reflexiveness. It has been entirely overlooked. In the old we paid no attention to it.

All I said applies to language, that is why I am using a map for an example. The '*word*' is not the '*fact*'. Yet we act as if it were. Then a word does *not* cover *all* characteristics of a fact or a situation. So, you see it applies to language. And finally, comes the *self-reflexiveness*, a source of permanent difficulties and identifications, because *in* language we can speak *about* language. You will see later on in application to life of what great importance that fact is. Here is a story of a barber. There was only one barber in a small town, and he shaved only those who did not shave themselves. Then the problem was "Did the barber shave himself?" Now,

Lecture Four

do you realize that whenever we are talking about a self-reflexive problem, we get into the barber problem? Whatever you say you are wrong. Whether you say "yes" or "no" you are always wrong. And that is what happens with self-reflexive problems. So-called human intelligence ceases to act. You cannot be intelligent when whatever you say is wrong. Where is your intelligence working, in fact where is your intelligence when you touch a problem that whatever you say is wrong? That is not a happy situation. We have to be forewarned about self-reflexive problems but they still remain one of the greatest dangers in our lives. These dangers have ruined the foundations of mathematics. Later on you will automatically take care of this self-reflexiveness through a very simple technique, and you will be able practically to avoid any difficulty over self-reflexiveness by the use of some very simple devices.

There came a question of whether our language is similar in structure to this world and ourselves, or not. Remember this is not a question of speculation. Speculation has nothing to do with it. It is a question of investigation of the facts. We have investigated facts and language. Curiously enough a great many people have spoken about it, but nobody until GS has made a thorough investigation of the subject. In the meantime life is going on and science is progressing, but they are not coordinated. Examine it. Remember you cannot divide 'matter', 'space', and 'time'. You cannot in the physical fact, but you can divide them verbally. Thus they are not similar in structure. But should we quit? No, page Einstein, and produce a language of space-time and we have a language of non-elementalistic structure. The facts are non-elementalistic and the language happens to be elementalistic. Otherwise, the existing language is not similar in structure to the facts and there is nothing to do about that but to revise the language structurally to a non-elementalistic basis. Then we will get a similarity of structure and therefore, predictability. I have to stress that. I have also to stress as a most important point, that the great achievements of science are due to the terminology of science. Never forget that.ABolish terminology and you have abolished the sciences. In the standard Oxford dictionary we find good English words that we never use, but they play the role of scientific terminology. When I speak to you I do not use any queer words, I use Standard English. But, there are terms that I will not use, because I would 'hang' myself if I did use them. But you are using terms that are definitely harmful.

As scientific people, I advise you definitely when you deal with a problem; test your language to begin with to see if it is a language that is elementalistic. For the facts are non-elementalistic. When you find your language is elementalistic, drop it, and find a term that would be non-elementalistic. That is definite advice and you will see that in non-elementalistic language you will have different results. Take examples, "thinking" and "feeling", "emotion" and "intellect", etc., are *elementalistic*. Just try to talk and do the things covered by a term "emotion" or "intellect". They imply separated entities, when as a matter of fact, the living actualities cannot be separated. As far as facts are concerned, you cannot divide 'emotion' and 'intellect'. Why speculate on *elementalistic* language then? Take the term *semantic reac-*

Lecture Four 59

tion which involves an evaluating reaction, that applies to your 'emotions'. It applies to the so-called 'intellect'. The term "semantic reaction" is non-elementalistic. Is it clear that instead of using "emotion" and "intellect", we should use "*semantic reaction*", which means evaluation and it applies to both. Otherwise that term is non-elementalistic. But, this is still not the worst of it.

Here I will introduce two new terms, and you have to be thoroughly familiar with those terms. These terms are not really new. They were known to Aristotle 2,300 years ago, but were never applied to life. The first term is *intension*, and I forewarn you the spelling must be with an "s" and not with a "t" because this changes the whole meaning. It is a technical term known to Aristotle and it means definition by aristotelian properties. It is an aristotelian definition by properties. An example, Plato, I think it was, defined "man" as a featherless biped. Now it makes no difference how we define a "man", we can define him as well as a featherless biped. You in this room are supposed to be so-called human beings. None of you has feathers. None of you has three legs. Then the definition featherless biped does apply to the whole class. Let's investigate further. We agreed that this verbal definition applied to *everyone*, now let's see whether it covers *anyone*. These people in front of me each have something different. The definition does not say that. Featherless biped does not say that. That definition does not cover anybody. What is your orientation if you go by definition? If you go by verbal fiction what kind of life orientation have you when important factors are left out of the definition? That is the danger of orientation by intension, by verbal definitions based on 'properties'.

Imagine that I have a terrible temper and that I am a thoroughly nasty fellow. That would not appear in the verbal definition of a featherless biped. One of you gets married by definition, and then next is Reno because you have married a definition but you have to live with the living being. You see, this goes so close to life. You must realize we live, and orient ourselves in the old way by verbalisms and definitions, but that does not cover all characteristics. This is intensional orientation. Then comes *extensional* orientation and *extensional* definitions.

Extensional definition is more than a definition; extensional orientation is exclusively mathematical and semantic, as such. Remember, there are two ways of treating the subject, one is definition by *intension* and the other, mathematical and semantic, is the orientation and definition by *extension*. Those terms are technical terms and have to be taken just as they come. The old stuff is intensional and the new is extensional, a complete departure from the old. By and by you will see the consequences of the application of it. By extension if you ask me to define "man" the definition would be in terms of a "class of individuals made up of $Smith_1$, $Smith_2$, $Smith_3$, etc." I exhibit individuals, label them, give them a proper name, but basically I exhibit *individuals*. This is a great departure from the old. This is not a fiction; it is a cultural necessity. It is a method of orientation in terms of 'reality'. Fancy I will take you as a class and talk about you. Each one of you is different. You are convinced of that. No matter what I will say about each, I could write an encyclopedia about the class; I would never cover any *one* of you. I cannot go, then, by verbal definition. But when I deal with you as

Smith$_1$, Smith$_2$, Smith$_3$, etc., as a class, a group, when I speak of individuals, then I am on the safer side. That makes the whole difference.

Now mathematics is fundamentally extensional. The mathematician deals only with his 'individual' numbers. No mathematician ever was interested in the problem of the definition of number. It is a problem for the foundation of mathematics, yes, but that is a different subject. No mathematician bothers about the definition of numbers. He is interested in the *behavior* of his individuals so that when he adds one to one he gets two. He is interested in individuals. Three minus two equals one. That is the behavior of individuals. They study the behavior of their individuals. This is why mathematics is extensional. The units of mathematics are such that they alone allow perfect generalities by intension and definition, but this exists only in mathematics. Nowhere else. Take a statement, one apple and one apple equals two apples. Don't be confused that I speak of such simple matters. These are the problems of the foundations of mathematics and they are very important. When you say one apple and one apple equals two apples that is not a mathematical statement. That is a physical statement. But when you say one and one equals two, that is mathematical. Mathematics represents only verbal patterns revealing also methods of analysis. We build them up, file them away, and then someone may use them.

The book *Topological Psychology* is mathematical, based only on how a part enters into a whole. Before, this was an abstract discipline. No one believed it would have any application; but today we have applied this to 'psychology' and later this may be applied to sociology, economics, politics, government, etc. All the time it is strictly a mathematical discipline. The more you see what has been done the more you enlarge your vision. The mathematics in *Topological Psychology* applies to all human problems as well as 'psychological'. The method is extensional. There are places in the book which are practically copies of my seminars, although the author probably had never heard of them. The method is the same.

Now I will give an example that is quite workable. You define "man" by intension by any of his properties. You must realize that it covers nobody, but the definition of man by extension as a class made up of $Smith_1$, $Smith_2$, $Smith_3$, etc., covers individuals. Don't forget that *Smith* part; that is important too. In the seventeenth century we have had mathematics developed, and for further progress we needed an infinite number of symbols. To supply these, mathematicians invented a trick: X_1, X_2, X_3, etc., then they had their indefinite number of symbols and so they solved their problems. The solution is extensional. Have you gotten the difference between intension and extension? Intension is based on verbalistic definition by properties, but by extension we exhibit the individuals and an orientation by individuals. I will give you an example of how it works.

Let's suppose you are all intensional because you were born and bred in an intensional world. (That is the difficulty of this work; I must train you away from that. It takes a great deal of training to become extensional. Then you belong to a new world that is extensional, made up of facts not definitions.) One of you says to me, "Cars are useful." That is a simple statement. I am extensionalized. What happens to me? I hear what you said, "Cars are useful." But I get this: "Car$_1$, Car$_2$, Car$_3$, etc., are useful." That is the way I react to "All cars are useful." I orient myself in terms of actual cars, not in definitions of a "car". And look what happens. Just because I visualize Car$_1$, Car$_2$, Car$_3$, etc., are useful, because I was analyzing in terms of *actual cars*, I 'see' poor brakes, drunken drivers, etc., which are not in your definition. You see, I think in terms of individuals which are not in your definition; and so to your statement that all cars are useful my reaction would be, "do you not believe that your statement is a little too broad, because some cars are harmful?" There is 'profound wisdom' in such a statement. You said cars are useful, and my reaction was 'car$_1$, car$_2$, car$_3$,' etc., but then I saw that the *actualities* did not fit your statement, then I made a remark that perhaps your statement was a little too broad. Try to get the 'broad wisdom' of this remark although the example is trivial. This is a simple example, but the fact is that I have limited your generality because I have made a careful statement where yours was too broad and I seem wise. Now that is the benefit of extension. It deepens you inwardly. It makes you face 'reality' and, as such, by 'facing reality', we are on a road to adjustment and sanity. It is nothing but adjustment really. You have probably heard something about psychiatry, 'mental' illnesses, and psychotherapy. Psychotherapy produces remarkable results, but it is still today largely a problem of individual skill.

The 'mental' health service of the University of Chicago utilizes GS, and we find in GS general methods for group psychotherapy because we extensionalize in principle, and we have a *general theory* of evaluation, which is a *general theory* of sanity. What psychotherapists do is nothing but drive the patient down to 'reality', down to the facts; which amounts to some sort of extensionalization, but without having a general theory, which GS supplies.

So, when you get thoroughly extensionalized you will see how a great many artificial difficulties will disappear. The questions I will raise are very simple, but very profound. I will show only a few examples. Contemplate this objective stick, the *word* "stick" which labels my cane and an indefinite number of other canes. The *word* "stick" represents only a definition and a fiction. This applies to everything, all of it by definition, all of it by verbal *fiction*. Do you like a word like that, and do you like to orient yourselves by fiction? Now in the meantime we have to talk. You would call that stick by extension, $stick_1$, others $stick_2$, $stick_3$, etc. You see, when we say "$stick_1$", we are dealing with a proper name, for an individual and then the word stick without index stands for a definition. I want to rub that in. The words "stick", "house", "man", etc., for any thing represents a verbal definition, otherwise a fiction. The moment you use them with indexes, you have *proper names* for *actual individuals* and you no longer deal with definitions. This is fundamental.

A definition by intension is by properties. But your definition by properties will never cover individuals. Then it is not safe to have a definition by properties. There is a great danger in this. Now a definition by extension would be a definition exhibiting the individuals. You can always think of that example as I told you that *man* by intension was defined as a featherless biped, and then by extension I exhibited a class of individuals, $Smith_1$, $Smith_2$, $Smith_3$, etc. Then I gave you the example about the cars. "Cars are useful." That is what you said. My reaction is "Car_1, car_2, etc., are useful." I orient myself in terms of individuals, and then drunken drivers, etc., come in. And then I make that very 'wise statement', "Don't you believe your statement is too broad?" It takes a lot of beating before people begin to see that. By extension you will get that wisdom without that beating.

Now I tell you of what I call *extensional devices*. There are five of them:

1) Indexes   4) Quotes
2) Dates   5) Hyphens
3) Etc.

Those are what I call extensional devices. They have to be used. That is the main difficulty; they have to be used *permanently* as a new type of reaction. You are not slowed down by being extensional. You see me here; I am not slowed down. But I cannot orient myself in *terms* of a 'chair' or a 'man', etc. To me everything is indexed. I don't 'think' of you as a "man" or a "girl", but as $Smith_1$, $Smith_2$, etc. It does not slow me down at all, but it makes me 'think' deeper. That is the art of 'thinking', because you orient yourself in terms of 'reality' all the time, not in terms of fictitious definitions. You will get the habit of it, and then the benefit of it.

As we live in a world of processes you are never 'the same', not even since you came here. You are getting a little bit older, etc. You are not the same. Now, probably most of you have sweethearts. Your sweetheart on Monday is not the same as your sweetheart on Tuesday. Nor is he the same in the morning as he is in the evening. Our toothache Monday is not the same as it is Tuesday. That is true about happiness too. When you use a date, you get much wisdom. I remember a pathetic case I was extensionalizing. The work was being done on a staff of a school and there were some very young girls in the class. Well, I had my seminars for the girls and had private conferences for a few of them. One had what may be called "inferiority complex". And when I was speaking about that inferiority complex, I asked, "Would you not enjoy to be as sure of yourself, etc., as I am?" She said she would. Then my next question was, "What do you think would happen if I would not date my statements permanently? What I say today I say today, and I do not legislate about tomorrow. Tomorrow I may have to change my opinion. If I did not *date my statements*, would I not be a perfect ass?" Because of unlimited security, only by the use of dates can we speak with security without dogmatism. I would be an ass if I did not use dates. Dates then abolish dogmatism. What I say today may be correct, for tomorrow I don't know. Dogmatism and absolutism are abolished permanently by the use of dates. If you make a statement with great security and if you date it, you have no 'cosmic legislation' for tomorrow. If I had made a statement about your dress being red and I had made this statement about your dress for all times to come, I would be a 'fool'. Look at our second premise, '*not all*'. By the use of dates we abolish dogmatism.

Lecture Four

Make a statement as strong as you wish but *date it* and you may be correct.

Let me draw your attention to another problem, that of the "et cetera". Every word must be indexed. Chair$_1$ is not the same as chair$_2$, etc.; everything has to be indexed, dated, and whenever you have a statement put on an "etc." so you will be conscious you have not stated 'all' or 'everything'. See the premise "*not all*". This connects directly with the "*is not*" premise.

Those first three extensional devices are what I call *working devices* and the fourth and fifth, quotes and hyphens, I call *safety devices*. In our old language, which we cannot readily change, it is extremely difficult to avoid elementalistic terms. This is why we have to use *quotes*. So when you speak and you use terms like "mind", you should use quotation marks. These are methods for actual practice. When you use terms like "mind" in quotation marks, you are using *safety devices*. When you use elementalistic terms for some practical reasons use them inwardly with quotation marks. Or if you speak about them, speak about them in quotation marks. Never speculate with or on elementalistic terms because it is worthless. Suppose I say your 'emotions' are aroused. I did not hesitate to say so, but inwardly I have used quotation marks with that. We have no right to speculate on elementalistic terms. Otherwise, if you have to use elementalistic terms, use quotation marks, then you will not speculate. Quotation marks eliminate that speculation. As you talk to the other fellow, you will confuse him if you use elementalistic terms without forewarning him of their unreliable character.

I wonder if you realize as a class that without those five devices which I shall call "our extensional bargain", I could not speak to you at all, honestly. I would speak only about definitions, verbal fictions, etc., and not actual entities, etc.; I am serious. In all honesty, without having between us that *bargain* there is not a human chance for us to talk sense. And, in all honesty, I could not speak to you at all. When we have the bargain between us, both with those five devices, then when I say "stick" it means between us, "$stick_1$, $stick_2$, etc." We are labeling 'realities' and orienting ourselves by 'realities'! Remember we are passing from an old intensional world to a new extensional world. It takes a great change in the character of orientations yet this change is beneficial and sane. As you will hear further, you will notice that I never preach. You do not notice any inclination in me for preaching. Preaching is useless. However, in life endless troubles appear. But by extension most of those troubles disappear. The old troubles turn out often to be due to *intension* and when we become *extensionalized* they automatically vanish.

Here we have a definite something to go by. We have those devices which are workable and you must apply them. I want to give you examples from life, how it works. In one school there was a Scotch teacher, and she was teaching her pupils a game of dancing in a circle. One person is in the center and the others dance around until the person in the center kisses one of the others. Then the kissed one takes the place in the center. Well, some child kissed the teacher, and so the teacher had to go inside the circle. It was then her turn to kiss one of the children. And, she knew that no matter what child she kissed, the other children would be unhappy. Playing on the mechanisms of unhappiness in a child is dangerous as we may later on produce some neurotic, so the teacher stood still and kissed automatically the child in front of her. Three or four others began to cry because they though[t] the teacher did not "love them". This is serious, because here we are dealing with the mechanism of unhappiness in a child. Well, the teacher gave this account to me. She indexed $kiss_1$, $kiss_2$, $kiss_3$, etc., and gave the children an explanation in terms of differences. She did not yell the indexes to the children. She told them that there are *different* kinds of kisses, and that they would all be kissed with a love kiss because the teacher loved them all, but in the game, the game kiss was automatic to whoever stopped in front of her. And all unhappiness disappeared. The indexing did it. So reported the teacher.

I will give you an example of the date now. When you have a little unpleasantness, date it, because, if you hold your grudges forever, you will not be a happy person. But if you know that somebody is angry, date that and disregard it, for he may not be angry tomorrow. After one seminar I came home with a married couple. When we came to my apartment the automatic elevators did not work, so we had to walk up six flights of stairs. In front of my door was the stairway and the elevators. When the people left at two in the morning they took to the stairs immediately, but I remembered to date. The elevator at twelve *was not* the elevator at two. I tried the elevators and they worked. They rode instead of walking down. It was so simple, but so important.

Today parent-child troubles are overrunning the world. Imagine that that fellow is my "father", now I hate him because he hurt me. Now I am speaking about tragic mechanisms. Life after life is ruined by these mechanisms. Watch what happens. That fellow who is my "father", he as the *individual* hurt me; but *I* hate (being extensional) Smith$_1$. I do not hate all "fathers". And I will not become psychotic or neurotic. I will not hate "all fathers". I want you to get that very important point. For example, a fellow was hurt in life in connection with a golf ball. Whenever he saw a golf ball, or heard of one, he was upset and incapacitated for a month. He was out of adjustment to golf balls. He was ruined, almost a suicide. This is an actual case. Whenever he saw a golf ball he went into a complete 'mental' collapse lasting for a long time. He was cured by extensionalization. And, the process consisted of consciousness that ball$_1$ is not ball$_2$, is not ball$_3$, etc. It took three or four months of steady work to help him, but that is what extensionalization did. He should not feel badly about every golf ball if a particular ball$_1$ had done something to him. He was cured because he was extensionalized and an intensional ball was the source of the illness. Reactions to one ball he revived with all balls. And by extensionalization he was cured. This is a standard mechanism which applies to all those indexes and those dates, and etc. You will get more of this later.

Now, do you understand the use of the extensional bargain? I want to show the hyphens in the few minutes still remaining with us. They should be used permanently to secure a new orientation. I will begin with fiction and we will try to make that more and more 'real'; and I want you to do this in your life. Say I put quotation marks to begin with around the word, "industry". There is a fiction there. Now how can we make it more 'real'? By using an index, industry$_1$. Then we date it, industry$_1$^{1937}. Each time we get closer to 'reality'. Then we use a hyphen, such as "industry$_1$^{1937}-in action". That is less of a fiction. Then add *demand* for goods as "industry$_1$^{1937}-in action-demand for goods". Of course, we could keep this up indefinitely, but if I put a period, I have made a perfect fiction. We must put '*etc.*' at the end of this chain of factors. When the use of the devices becomes habitual we are getting broad minded, deep, etc. Then you are gathering more factors of importance, because we are not stopped by factors of little importance. Another problem of evaluation.

SEMINAR LECTURE FIVE

As usual I will start tonight with a short summary of what we have already covered. From now on, however, it will not be necessary to put in the notes all that I say in this summary. But, I wish you would get the importance of *predictability*. When we cross a bridge don't we feel the inward sense of security, of predictability that that bridge will not fall in? Don't you feel a sense of security here in this building that the roof will not fall in on you? A sense of security, if you have predictability will you not have that security?

There is a branch of mathematics called the *theory of invariance*: invariance, meaning something that does not change. We have this in human affairs and even in mathematics. This involves unchanging values that give a sense of security. And we are made that way, so that security is what we want. You can see the connection between mathematical theory of invariance, lack of changeability, and the security of yourself, which all depend on predictability. Factors of predictability are not generally recognized, but they may be of importance in our private, national and international lives. The aim of science and mathematics is predictability. So if we can find the factors of predictability, we are getting at the very bottom of the factors of life and at the factors by which our personal problems are to be solved.

We have not covered all these factors in our map examples of the preceding lectures, but we are unraveling those a little and thus getting closer to sanity and a better white civilization. I say white civilization because I do not know whether GS will affect other races or not. We will have to wait and see. Otherwise we must investigate the facts. This is not very simple.

I told you, didn't I, about my optimism of pessimism? You know the ordinary English meaning of the word "optimism", and the word "pessimism". If you would say I am pessimistic or optimistic, it would really make no difference whichever you said because it is all nonsense anyway. Very often I am called by some people, a hopeless optimist. Now I want to clarify those words "optimism" and "pessimism". This applies to many other words of that sort. If I had a sick liver, and if I had gone around the world saying "that is bad. That is bad, and that is bad", I would have been a pessimist. I didn't do that though, for I did not have a sick liver. But I looked around, and because I had a healthy liver, I came to the conclusion that the world is not 'bad' — just *hopeless*. But if we know we have problems before us we can always solve them. So when we believe that a situation is hopeless, it would have been 'bad' according to the old. But we can always *solve* the *hopeless* in the new. The moment we face a situation frankly, a solution appears. This is true about the whole history of civilization. I will give you a mathematical example.

Savages and children can solve equations of the first order. If you have three apples and someone takes away one, you have two left. The new orientations necessary are as clear as that. Most of our difficulties are man-made stupidities. When it comes to equations of the first order, they can be solved by children. Then, an equation of the second order requires about high school education, otherwise they are comparatively more difficult. It takes an advanced high school training to solve them. Then in the third and fourth degree equations we learn again how to solve them, though they are more difficult. After this. mathematicians made a rough generalization that *all* equations could thus be solved algebraically. This was important, for we needed to solve these equations; we needed them in our business. Then came a young fellow by the name of Galois, being young and a creative genius, he wondered about this. He was killed in a duel over a love affair, but the night before the duel he wrote what might be called a 'mathematical testament' in which he proved that equations above the fourth order could not be solved algebraically. You remember that the general assumption was that they could be solved indefinitely. *Not all.* This fellow proved that equations above the fourth order cannot be solved at all. And what happened? Just because that situation was faced, he immediately invented the Theory of Groups by which you can solve any equations.

I want you to get that, when a situation is formulated and that is faced, frankly, we always know how to solve it. But before a solution can come, we have to face the insolubility of the old stuff. There is a connection between that and health. I want you to get it because this is only a technical example out of the history of science.

I am not sick, and so I looked over the world and came to the belief that the old is unsolvable. So we found a solution. There is a cultural connection between this and the mathematical theory of groups. Now, the question, "Am I an optimist or pessimist?" has no sense. Because I start with the bottom of pessimism when I say that the problem is insolvable and just because of that we reach a solution. Then the solution in turn becomes optimistic. That is merely "masturbation of the salivary glands". Let us talk facts clearly, not make "noises".

We have a lot of noises today in the 'philosophies'. They are based on the many questions and 'noises' which mean nothing and there is nothing to be known about them. The only answer to them is to say with a broad Oxford accent, "Dear fellows, you make noises". If you clear up in your orientation and discriminate 'noises' from *words*, a great many difficulties will clear up. Many students make mistakes in translation of the new terms into the old in that they fail to realize *you must have a known element in structure*, and that new terms involve new structural assumptions absent in the old. Now let me say to you in connection with gravity and Einstein that structure has to be based on related groups of structural formulations. This is similarity of structures. That is mathematical relation, too. That is the connection between mathematics, mathematical methods, and language. We hide in language; we will seek method. By method, we mean the way white human brains respond to stimuli of the world. The answer to it is a problem of method. It is how the human brain responds to stimuli.

Lecture Five

The whole white civilization is facing a disaster. Why? Because we are living in an actual world made by extensional science while our linguistic orientations remain intensional. You know how the motorcar, the radio, and the aeroplane have revolutionized our lives. Now you may not know it, but you cannot build that motorcar, or that radio, or that aeroplane by Euclid or Newton. When electricity comes in they will not work. Otherwise the actual conditions under which we live are already affected by *non-newtonian* and *non-euclidean* disciplines. Whether you like it or not does not matter. You can build a house by Euclid or Newton, but you cannot build a motorcar. Can you live sanely with Aristotle under the conditions of non-euclidean and non-newtonian character? This is why we need a revision of the old orientation which would fit the new conditions of life that are already built by non-euclid and non-newton. This revision comes in GS. The methods are new, but the facts on which we base our methods are not new. They have just never been applied. I will explain more of this in my next lecture.

Now I want to go on to a sort of perfunctory analysis of the working of the nervous system. I could not have done that before because without the extensional devices it is humanly impossible to talk sense about the nervous system. I do not 'blah-blah' about it as we do otherwise, but I try to talk sense. I suggest very seriously that you read and even buy the book of Alexis Carrel, *Man the Unknown*. I urge you, the whole class to read it, and if you can, buy it. Carrel is a world famous physician. Nobel prize winner, etc., one of the greatest men we have. This is an epoch making book. People could say that *I* am slandering medicine, because I have not the authority to talk that way. But Carrel has, and he gives them a lesson. He tells them to begin with, that which I treat as a matter of fact, is valid. True, he disregards linguistic issues. He is perfectly unaware of the semantic environment. What he calls 'schemata' we call here *verbal fictions*, but we are both protesting against the same things. Try to fancy the actual facts. The colds you have are not one thing and each of you does not have that one thing. They are individual things applying to the whole. They are not the same. But when you talk intensionally in terms of definitions about some ailments, say a cold, you are talking about a fiction. A primitive man has an ordinary cold and is taken to a white hospital, and he dies. The cold did not kill him. No, rather fear of unknown conditions. The semantic environment of a savage in a white hospital killed him. You should be getting more or less familiar with the importance of the semantic environment and evaluation. You must realize that the majority of sex trouble has nothing to do with the anatomical side of it. It is in the head. Semantic environment, and linguistic environment Carrel disregards, yet he is calling for the 'science of man', which this disregard makes impossible.

But, overlooking the semantic and linguistic environment we cannot build up a science of man. Remember that what we are doing is disinfecting our brain, realizing the natural possibilities in us. All we can do is to eliminate the vicious fictions. Later on you will understand better how that is done. The difficulty is very fundamental, a difficulty with which you will have to struggle to work out.

Lecture Five

Tonight I want to talk to you about the nervous system. The difficulty here is called in neurological terms, *canalization*. This has other names, such as "Bahnung" (railroading), and another, the law of facilitation. This is a general neurological aspect which applies to us as well as to animals. We consider fibers in our nervous systems, say fiber A is there, and we have an impulse A' which passes through that fiber A, and there comes another impulse X' which should pass through fiber X. It will not though. It will come through the *more traveled* fiber A. This is a general characteristic of the nervous system. This is what we call 'canalization', or 'facilitation' or 'Bahnung'. This is a fundamental fact of the working of the nervous system. Our ability for habit formation, for learning, etc., depends on the fact that we can train some fibers to take the impulses in preference to other fibers. If some trained fibers would not have the preference for passing impulses, that would hinder education. Otherwise that characteristic of canalization is the neurological foundation of education and habit formation.

Now, because of that there are difficulties in acquiring extensional orientations and extensional habits, because we are canalized in the old way. This goes back to the nervous system. Now here comes the great difficulty. We are trained from childhood in intensionalism, so this is a neuro-semantic problem which you will all have to overcome. You will have to overcome the old canalization. I went personally through three recanalizations. I was trained in good old Aristotle and Euclid, and good old Newton. Then I began to look around at non-euclidean systems, and non-newtonian systems (Einstein, etc.), and finally formulated a non-aristotelian system.

When you take up a textbook of euclidean geometry, the one you are all familiar with, no matter where you look, the end or the beginning, you find yourselves at home. But when you take a textbook of non-euclidean geometry the beginning will sound quite innocent but it will not be familiar very long. I might as well explain this to you. You should know about non-euclidean principles.

In all metric geometries we need lines which never meet. We must have them. Because we need them, we have made them. We call them "parallels". Now here comes a certain point about those parallels that is interesting. We need those lines that never meet. We have to have them. We cannot have a geometry without them. But then Euclid setting down his geometry, defined those 'parallels' as not only not meeting, but he put another condition on those lines, that they were *equal distance apart*. Even in the time of Euclid, though, that equal distance business was challenged. People did not feel at home with those parallels. Mathematicians knew even in the days of Euclid that there might be lines that never meet and yet were not of equal distance. But, Euclid said equal distance. This bothered mathematicians for more than 2,000 years, and finally three men, all at one period, challenged this principle. They simply said to themselves, "Let's not argue, let's produce a geometry where we have lines which never meet and yet are not of equal distance." And, they were told that they were fools. Their works were published as non-euclidean geometries where parallel lines never meet, but they are not said to be of equal distance. You have noticed all the nice curves that things about us are made up of. You have seen some of the old apartment houses that are made of such straight euclidean parallel lines that they somehow are repulsive.

Today as a result of this non-euclidean principle we believe that there are no straight lines in the world at all. In the old days our circles or curves were the limit made up of short bits of 'straight' lines. When you had a great many short lines you finally got a curve. Otherwise, a curve in the Euclid days was made up of bits of straight lines. Today we assume differently. If we take a circle of a very small radius it is very curved. If you take a larger radius, the curve is flatter. Finally, if you took the limit of a circle of an infinite radius you would have what is called a straight line. In the old days we made curves out of small bits of straight lines. Today, the straight lines are nothing but a limit of a curve of infinite radius. Only a reversal, but the orientation is different.

What I want you to understand is the complete revision of the orientation we are carrying on, in mathematics and in life. It is a great difference, whether we made a curve out of bits of straight lines or whether we make straight lines today as the limiting case of a curve of an infinite radius of curvature. This is important for all of you. It is the reverse of the whole thing, a complete reversal. This is very important. It has been shown by behavior and by actual facts that the equal distance is not necessary, and the non-euclideans have abolished that one simple assumption by producing an actual geometry where that postulate is left out, and yet, they produced a self-consistent geometry. Today you will find in addition that nothing electrical follows Euclid or Newton. And don't you forget that we are nothing but electrical structures. When you look at it, if you see a textbook of non-euclidean geometry, the first two pages will appear familiar, but believe me, the third and fourth page will be completely new. You are lost. You are thoroughly unfamiliar with it because of your old canalization.

Now it turns out that Euclid is *not similar in structure* to the world, because we don't know straight lines and we don't have lines of equal distance in the world today. We deal only with curves today. In Euclid, with his straight lines which are non-existent, there is no similarity of structure to the world as we know it. The non-euclidean geometries in science today are all based on curves and their limiting values which may be called straight lines, just as you wish. That "as you wish" is an important point. All the 'facts' are just "as you please". The 'facts' remain but they may be interpreted differently. So we may say that the new geometry is based on curves not straight lines. We don't talk about straight lines. We talk about the shortest line (geodesics), which we may then assume to be 'straight', but we don't talk of them as straight lines.

Euclid as a formulation then was not similar in structure to the facts as we know them. This is empirical. Euclid's geometry is not similar in structure to the facts of the world. As far as principles are concerned, it is not similar, and we have to abandon it in principle. I will

Lecture Five   83

show you later that Newton's mechanics is not similar in structure to the world too. The whole seminar will stress that the old intensional beliefs are not similar in structure to the facts. I will not go into Newton tonight, but later. I only want to cover the nervous system tonight.

Carrel again is criticizing science and medicine men (I will not call them medical men) because they deal with verbal schemes which they fancy as actualities. They deal with 'organs', but in the living being we have only functional units. And, we cannot separate them. If I split the nervous system, anatomically, I do not talk sense, I just make noises. I make noises because you cannot really split them, as all of them are connected *functionally*. There is no such thing as '*cortex*' separated from function even at an instant in Smith$_1$. At an instant in a given person function can be localized but how can we speak under such conditions without extensional devices. All parts of the nervous system are interconnected functionally. We cannot speak about such a situation without indexing and dating. At an *instant* in a given individual you may say something valid, but we cannot speak about it intensionally. Remember what I will say now about the nervous system is elementary knowledge, but the way I will express it is fundamentally wrong because I will speak, as we have to, in elementalistic terms which disregard function and the instantaneous cross-section in a given individual. What I will say is fundamentally wrong, but *partially true*. But if we keep the extensional bargain we will be able to talk sense and have a glimpse at very complex situations. So now I will speak in the old fashioned way. In the meantime we have to know and keep our extensional bargain for safety so that we will not go too far astray. Remember all I say is only approximate, depending on the instant of my speaking, about a given individual.

One part of the nervous system can take up the work of another. We can speak on those subjects exclusively by using indexes and dates. A surgeon may tell you he can put out of business your little finger. Today he may do that, tomorrow he may not do that, and his statement is in principle incorrect. The function of the nervous system *is* largely *interchangeable*. Another nerve may make the finger work tomorrow. Today we graft wires into the brain and study brain waves. They are different at different times, and in different sexes and in each individual. The old was based on generalization, verbal schemes, etc., but the new takes into account four-dimensional individuality. In four dimensions we have only individuals and everything is different. In the old days we did not pay attention to it, but the facts remain.

Then we have what we call the "cortex", the upper layer of the brain, and we as humans have more cortex than any other being. The approximately central part of the brain is called the thalamus and it is directly connected with the outside world through the 'senses', largely connected with 'emotions', 'pain-pleasure', etc. I use quotation marks with all of this. And, remember what I am saying is false because I am speaking in parts, when the whole works as a *whole*. We have to use that extensional bargain between us so that I will not misguide you. The parts interplay permanently functionally, but I have to speak as if they did not.

LECTURE FIVE 85

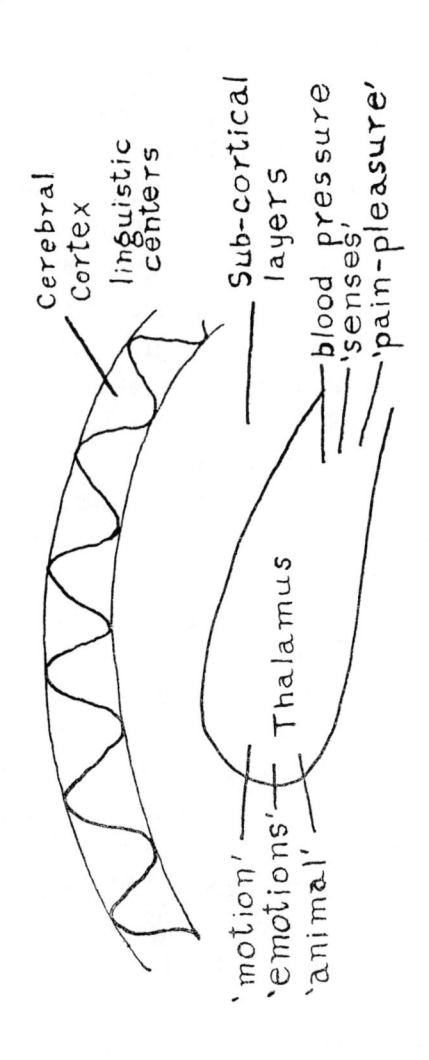

Cerebral Cortex

linguistic centers

Sub-cortical layers

blood pressure
'senses'
'pain-pleasure'

Thalamus

'motion'
'emotions'
'animal'

Every part of the nervous system is in permanent functional connection with, say, another one. Now, linguistic centers are in the 'cortex'. And then there is a permanent interplay of the functioning of the 'cortex' and the functioning of other parts of the brain, particularly the 'thalamus'. Now the question is what is the relative importance of the interplay between the 'cortex' and the 'thalamus'? To begin with, we know that the eye is not a so-called 'sense' organ. Embryology shows us that the brain develops and pushes out from itself the eye. Otherwise, the eye is an actual part of the brain. It is the outside part of the brain. This is why visual knowledge and orientations are of the most important forms of our orientations. This is why 'all' the instruments of science depend on the eye. You cannot trust anything else but the eye. Because the eye is part of the brain, one of the benefits of GS is that we formulate everything to the eye. I started with maps because then we are dealing directly with the brain through the eye.

Later you will see that animals are more 'ear-minded' than 'eye-minded', and you will see that intensional 'ear-mindedness' is not the highest grade of human intelligence or orientations. An intensional fellow is obviously 'ear-' and not 'eye-minded'. The extensional fellow will be 'eye-minded'. You can see how far this distinction goes. And this is the passing from the old animalistic 'ear-minded' intensional era to the new civilization which will be 'eye-minded' and therefore extensional. The main problem is to produce new extensional means and methods for such visualization, which we try to produce in GS.

SEMINAR LECTURE SIX

To begin with, I wish you would all take this material a little more seriously. These things are of value only to yourself; I cannot live your life for you, you must do this yourself. That is why you must get this material by yourself. I want to scold you for not treating your life and your brain better than you do. You go to a dentist for your teeth, why don't you attend to your brain and your life then? You have to attend to your brain; it will not work by itself. Don't fancy that the present education system is satisfactory either. It is criminal, not satisfactory. Your staff here at Olivet is trying to do the best it can under the 'old' system. Education is increasing dementia praecox in America under the present system of presentation. Without the fundamentals of what I tell you, which is mathematical and physical, there can be no sanity. That is why GS is so important. Today education looks at mathematics and physics and says they are good enough but they are not very interesting. But, if you still live in the old you are ready for a hospital. When your kidneys are sick you consult a specialist and attend to them. Your brain is not less important. Why then don't you pay more attention to it? Mathematics and physics are the bases to train yourself on. You must pay more attention to the basic importance of these physico-mathematical methods. This is the criminal part of modern education. Mathematics and physics are neglected and further pushed away. Without a better foundation of mathematics and physics the problem of the *neurological deterioration* of the people of the United States of America cannot be solved.

What I will speak about tonight will deal with this. It will deal with this situation as a matter of fact. Don't forget that all I say is a matter of fact. Investigate, look into facts, do not blind yourself by false fictions.

When you become extensionalized you will be living on an entirely different planet. You will be in a different world from the rest. Actually! You are thus set aside from the rest. But, there is this to compensate you: You can understand the other fellow, but the other fellow cannot understand you.

Remember our extensional bargain. When I say something, you should index it. You must do this to limit it to the context in which I say it. My statements, and any statements, are worthless verbiage when taken out of their context, out of the 'environment' in which they were said and made operative. By indexing statements, not only words, you are prepared for this. To give you an example of this I will give you an extensional theory of happiness. That theory is in a way final because it is based *only* on extensional clarifications and I may add that the diagram of happiness, which I will show you, has high psychotherapeutic value and by now is used by some psychiatrists with patients. Remember, quotation marks are used to cover 'facts' in their contexts too. 'Facts' themselves mean nothing, but only in a context are they valuable. 'Facts' in a context, meaning a situation, etc., have value.

A combination of relationships that applies to what we say constitutes the context of 'fact' and gives it meaning or values. The interrelation of relation in a context gives a 'fact' its value. If you don't consider these relationships of the context, the 'facts' mean nothing (no value). Well, here then we have a number of facts in quotation marks, and then comes our problem of evaluation, individual or the one which was given to us which ultimately turns out to involve expectation based on some standards of values. This is the happiness formula again. Remember that this analysis is only possible by extension. By intension you could not do it.

This is already an application of extensional method. Now here comes our expectations. Here are some 'facts', any kind of 'facts' ('F'). I call the new, expectation$_2$ (E_2). Remember that this analysis can be made only by *extension*, not by *intension*. Now, you expect, in regard to the facts of life, say, 'nothing' (minimum). That is you are told to expect minimum. What will we *find* in actual *life*? You will find the facts *better* than you expected. Remember you were taught to expect the minimum. You will find that the *facts in life* will actually be better because you expected nothing. Then your reactions or evaluations would be "'facts' are *better* than I expected", that will react on the living you, encouraging you, etc., to happier living. Say I expect five students here and find seventy-five. I got more than I expected. The interest is better. The facts are better than I expected. And I am happy then. I feel like working ahead in the world where I expect five and get seventy-five. This applies to every one of you, in every phase of life. If you expect, say 'nothing', in the actual living, bumping against facts, impact with the environment, you will find the facts better than you expected. You will be encouraged. You will not be cynical; you will not be bitter; etc. Life then will be happier for you as living protoplasm reacting to the impact of the environment. Expect the minimum. That is expectation$_2$ (E_2). That is the new extensional infinite-valued expectations based on maximum probability.

Finding the facts *better* than you expected, you will be cheerful, you will be hopeful, you will be striving for a better end in your life just because you *expected* minimum, and will become convinced that you can get the maximum and you most likely will succeed.

Now the old way often ruins people and only brings about unhappiness, neurosis and even psychosis. Expectation$_1$ expects too much. If you expect too much, or maximum, the 'facts' will appear worse to you. In the old we are educated to *expect too much*. Our parents, educators, etc., expect too much. They nag life out of us and make psychotics or neurotics out of us. Now here comes the impact of the environment. As you see I do not change the 'facts' on the diagram at all. Say I expected five hundred students and I get seventy-five. I would not get my expectation and I would be unhappy. When you expect too much we find the facts worse. And, then we get cynical, frustrated, bitter, and whatnot. So you see, expect little or expect too much, you can see what it means in a living being. When you can evaluate life, knowing that there is no right for anybody to expect

EXTENSIONAL THEORY OF HAPPINESS
as part of neuro-semantic and neuro-linguistic environments

Old intensional expectations (E_1) based on two-valued aristotelian 'certainty', two-valued orientations:

New extensional expectations (E_2) based on maximum probability, infinite-valued orientation, etc.:

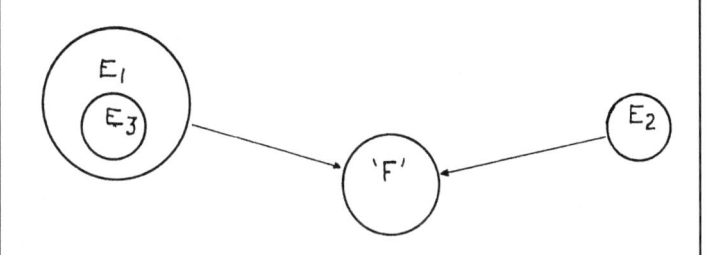

"Maximum expectation" (E_1). Actual living and impact of 'facts' will show that 'facts' are *worse* than expected results. Disappointment in life, cynical, bitter, frustrated, etc., lack of interest in life, asocial attitudes, often hostile, hopelessness, bitterness, etc., based on misunderstandings, false knowledge, etc., nagging, fearful, often hateful family, etc., relations. Hopeless, frustrated, etc., life orientations;
ETC.

"Minimum expectation" (E_2). Without suffering or punishment, actual living and impact of 'facts' will show that 'facts' are *better* than expected *results*. Interest in life, constructive curiosity, hopefulness, cheerfulness based on understanding, etc.;
ETC.,
ultimately quiet, civilized happiness and so adjustment and sanity;
ETC.

'Minimum expectations' (E_3). After much unnecessary suffering and punishment, similar verbiage as in (E_2), yet the living being Smith$_1$ is bitter, cynical, hostile, anti-social, revengeful, non-constructive, frustrated, etc., often a neurotic or psychotic, unhappy, no possibility for adjustment and sanity;
ETC.

too much, then we will all be better off in our lives and so be happier.

If I would expect too much, would I be disappointed? But if I know the difficulty, then I am not disappointed. I am very serious in this. Don't expect too much in living. If you take what I say on its level, I will accomplish a lot. But if you expect too much, my answer is the second premise, not all. Now here comes the crucial point of living, extensional living: that new expectation comes by extension without beating. This is a method that teaches you how to be happy without the beating. So you see this is a method of value. The benefit through a general theory of evaluation is 'mental' health without beating. When you are prepared for it, difficulties of life through methods of evaluation, you may be happy without the beating.

When you expect too much as we are trained in life, you will find the facts worse. You are cynical. That is the difference. When you expect too much, and you are beaten up, then comes what I call expectation$_3$, expecting nothing *after beating*. When life has stepped on you and you are all beaten up, you will get to expect nothing. But it is after beating. That is the difference. This is to expect nothing without beating, and to be prepared for the impact of environment and thus avoid shocks, or come to the conclusion to expect nothing after the beating. Here is an extensional analysis of a very important situation. Maladjustments are helped by this; sanity is made by it.

I want you to notice here that I say the same words but they have a different value in the different context, 'before or after beating'. This is coming back to the other point again in this same example. Expecting nothing in expectation₂ and expectation₃. They are the same words, but they do not mean the same. You have an entirely different outlook with the same words. I give you that as an example of how intensional words, when taken by extension, mean something entirely different. Disregard facts and live by intension and you will be quite unhappy — but the same fellow will be quite happy expecting nothing by extensional orientations. We could not have covered the same thing by intension that we did by extension. Remember the unhappy way is the old way. Don't be cynical as American youth is. American youth is spoiled from the bottom up. Parents, teachers, and preachers all educate you in the intensional way. Make life for your children happier; prepare them for the hardships they will find in life. Education should do this too. This is one of the great breaks between the old and the new.

The old aristotelian certainty and security went with the intensional too much expectation. The new non-aristotelian goes by the mathematical, maximum probability of predictability. Maximum probability of predictability. It is an infinite-valued orientation instead of the old two-valued certainty. We are coming to that new orientation in which the two-valued orientation is only a special case; 'either-or', 'good-bad', 'yes-no', that is two-valued orientation. I will ask any of you, "Are you all 'good'?" "Are you all 'bad'?" If you answered that question "good or bad" as "good", you would be wrong. If you answered "bad", you would be wrong, too. That is the whole difficulty of two-valued orientation. A hundred years ago they would burn me at the stake for saying that. You see the date of orientation does make a difference.

Now let's go back to the nervous system. You have a head and inside that is a brain. We and the animals all have a use for the head besides holding up our hats. Ask your biologist to tell you more about the amoeba than I will tell you here. But my example will bring us face to face with some of the difficulties of the old intensional language, difficulties that can be surmounted in the new, but not in the old. In other words, we cannot even be intelligent in the old way.

Now, when a little animal passes the amoeba it blows itself out into a neck and forms a sort of temporary mouth, and enwraps the animal, digests it, and then opens up and eliminates the remainder. But you cannot call this 'intelligent' neurological organization. The amoeba has no organs and no nervous system, yet she acts 'intelligently'. But her behavior was adequate for the amoeba. You would not be here if there had been no amoeba. You would not have your brains, if in this protoplasm there had been no possibilities for neuro-muscular-intelligent behavior. Now what happens next? As a prey moves close by, the amoeba kicks her protoplasm in a sort of temporary leg, follows the prey and swallows it. That is neuro-muscular-intelligent behavior too, but remember there is no nervous system nor muscular system in the amoeba, and *no brain*.

Here is another example. Do you know how a root of a squash can behave? These are facts. If you take a seedling of squash and grow it in a vessel that can be rotated, if you take that root and hang it crosswise, in ten minutes it would collapse. In nine minutes it does not.

Then put that root at nine-minute periods in all directions and you do that twenty or thirty times. After several days with nine-minute periods, the squash root will wiggle. The root learned the lesson. We trained the root. Actually trained a root.

I call the brain the "cosmic corn" because it has been produced by the impact of the environment. It is really our nervous system. The amoeba has no nerves or brain but when it becomes necessary for it to move there is a head end formed. The impact of the environment is at one end, and that forms the head end. And slowly we have what Professor Child calls "dynamic gradients" of degrees of responsiveness. This is how heads have happened. The head end becomes more and more sensitive and more responsive because of metabolic factors and more factors in evolution. That is the beginning of the nervous system. You know how the corns on your feet are made by the impact of the environment? The nervous system has been made from an amoeba up by the impact of the environment and we have followed from this. That impact of environment today has been changed, but we are still up against the new impact of environment. Today again, that impact of the environment is changed, the environment is changed, and we are not ready for it nervously. As a result of this. in America breakdowns are faster than in Europe. We are not ready to meet that new impact of environment, so the impact of environment brings a breakdown in the nervous system. Experiments have been made on low animals, especially sea animals, in which they have cut off these animals' nervous systems. But even with the nervous system cut they react just the same as before, only a *little slower*. This is a general condition. The time element enters into the nervous system, and they have discovered the main role of the nervous system is to accelerate reactions. That is where the sensitivity of the nervous system comes in. That goes from the lowest animals to the highest, and us. This is why our white civilization is going ahead so fast, because our 'cosmic corns' have the most accelerated action of all. This is why we progress. We can pile up achievements that the animals cannot, and yet we have part of our brain still not used. A large part of the cortex is not being used.

But now comes the tragedy of it all. Through the impact of environment the character of the metabolism of the protoplasm has changed. Originally accidental, then this became canalized and a head began to appear. That acceleration of response and action began to become structuralized and canalized and a head was formed, until Olivet and you and me. But when we speak that we sprang from the ape the facts of that show we did not 'spring' far enough. The world is made up of individuals. There is a view of a freak appearing in our families isn't there? You know of some freaks. They are bound biologically to occur in families. Then an ape of some sort had a freak in his family. That is how our ancestors came. From freak we went to freak until Einstein and you and me. All this is individual characteristics.

You do remember a grand symphony, a concert, but you do not realize the individuality of every instrument and the individuality of every player. This applies everywhere, life included. Now you get all the characteristics all the time, but sometimes they disappear because the conditions are not for survival. When a caterpillar goes to the top of the tree and eats leaves to later turn into a butterfly, the old way called this 'divine wisdom'.

In the new way we call this tendency of the caterpillar *positive heliotropism* and explain it on the basis of a chemical response to the presence of light. In an experiment we put the roots of a plant up and the leaves on the ground. But the 'divine wisdom' of the caterpillar caused him to still climb up and he starved and died. He had the leaves in front of him on the ground, but he climbed up and died. He was forced to respond to light and hence he climbed. Now there are probably caterpillars which are born negatively heliotropic. They do not survive. And there are some born probably that are neither negative nor positive heliotropic. That is where environment comes in. You can understand now why impact of the environment causes some characteristics to remain and some to disappear. There are some conditions which we can survive and some we cannot. To some we can adjust ourselves, and to some we cannot. Life is so complex in modern times that with the old orientations we cannot adjust ourselves to them. Hence we are breaking down. Can you see the total *intensional* adjustment you can make? You are not in touch with 'reality' by intension. You are closer to 'reality' by extension and you have a better chance to survive. There is not so much difference then between us and the survival adjustments of caterpillars. This is the application of the impact of the environment and it is the adjustment we have to make for ourselves by extension, not intensional orientations.

We are working at a cultural necessity, not just a fad. This is not a private fancy but a cultural necessity on which our whole adjustment depends. You can realize how the impact of environment was making us through a change of metabolism, through chemical reactions, through 'time' factors, and sensitivity, all that connects with them. The head emerged through the impact of environment. Get the joke of the 'cosmic corn' through impact of the environment? Now, I was telling you that in the lower animals when we cut the nervous system no fundamental change in their reactions took place.

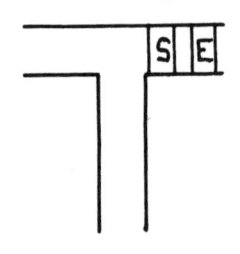

Now we can take a worm and make a T-maze and put in the one end of the maze an electrical bridge (E) with sandpaper (S) in front. When you take this earthworm and make him go, he gets a fair warning by contact with the sandpaper (S) before he gets to the electrical bridge (E) and gets shocked. But when he touches this he backs up quickly. And perhaps if you start him again, after some trials, he will go in the opposite direction, and will get no shock. In about eighty lessons he will go in that direction only. He will learn. Then cut off his head. And after his head is cut off you would expect all his learning to disappear. But still try him. He will go the 'right' direction without a head. It will take him a little longer, but he will still remember his lesson.

Otherwise, 'intelligence' is only *accelerated* by the nervous system and the brain. The brain plays the role of an accelerating device. When it comes to us with elaborate nervous systems complexities arise. You know we have a thalamus which is 'in direct contact with our environment', all in quotation marks because it cannot be divided from the rest. Here we have the cortex, which regulates the thalamus, and where the linguistic centers are. We have about six children on record, which were born without a cortex. With no cortex at all, they were not fit to live. They were a living bit of meat, nothing more. When I wrote my book we knew of only one such boy. After a year this boy began to cry permanently until he died at the age of three. Crying is mostly thalamic action so, after the age of one, the thalamus began to over-act because there was no cortex to control it. Before this there was no need for this particular regulating action of the thalamus by the cortex. The thalamus is in direct contact with the world so it is over-stimulated. Stimuli that go to the cortex pass through the thalamus. All living life is connected with the thalamus, which is over-stimulated and overworked, and cannot long stand the more and more increased stimulations which we find in daily life.

For sanity's sake we should pay attention to the protection of the thalamus. We could not have survived without a protecting organ like the cortex. That is the role of the cortex, particularly in modern life. Now, as the linguistic centers are in the cortex we can imagine such semantic and linguistic factors which instead of eliminating that over-stimulation of the thalamus, cause a condition where the cortex produces more stimulation to the thalamus. Then the cortex aids the over-stimulation and so augments maladjustment.

We should have semantic and linguistic conditions such that the cortex dampens down, slows down, and regulates the thalamus. *The center of intensional or extensional environment is in the thalamus or cortex. Approximately in the cortex.* Now as intensional and extensional semantic environment is largely cortical, intensional cortex training does not protect our thalamus. And, when we introduce extension, then the cortex begins to protect the thalamus. You understand the reason why extension plays a neurological role, helping to control the over-stimulation of the thalamus, which by the facts of life is over-stimulated. This is very important.

SEMINAR LECTURE SEVEN

*A*gain we will start with a summary of what we have covered. We live often by representations of 'facts' as much as by the 'facts'. Before we can act we must have some form of representation in our brains. Before you can sit on a chair you must have some form of representation of that chair in your brain and your nervous system. You act by those representations in your nervous system. And if they are not similar in structure to actual life your reactions will not be appropriate to the conditions of life. You cannot then be a successful and useful human citizen as you will not be happy. You should see the great importance in actual life to have your orientations similar in structure to the facts of life. Now let's generalize our three premises.

Let's generalize our first premise. Then we have: that a form of representation going on in our heads *is not* the outside fact. The chair you sit on *is not* the picture you have in your head of that chair. They are 'the same' only in your word. And they are only approximate and individual abstractions of the facts. If you are 'mentally' ill perhaps this chair upon which you sit will appear to you to be a knife. Your form of representation is entirely unsimilar in structure to the facts. If you were 'mentally' ill you might be afraid to sit on the chair because to you it is a knife. But it has not changed really. That is the broadness of this; this is where science and sanity come in.

Representing 'facts' as 'facts' and having a *map-language* that will correspond to 'facts', are equivalent to one another. This is the whole secret of 'insanity' and sanity. Our world is not governed by it yet, that is why we have such an unhappy world. This led us to the *law of non-identity*. There is no 'identity' in this world; but the whole old orientations are based on 'identity'. Insanity is based on identifications, identifications in a world where there is no *identity*. You will find in daily life endless serious problems produced by identifications, or improper evaluations.

Did you ever consider terms like "yes" and "no", "good" and "bad", "true" and "false", etc.? "Yes" has one meaning by intension, by definition. But suppose you say, "Yes, I want a smoke." That smoke is the actual extensional life content of this "yes". That is the life content of an extensional "yes". "Yes, I want a glass of water." Water then is the extensional content of this "yes_2". Extensionally they are different, intensionally 'the same'. The old "yes" was intensional but what I received and experienced was extensional. And they are not extensionally 'the same' yeses. We can distinguish between them by the extensional devices, "yes_1", and "yes_2", etc. This will apply very often in life. Many human troubles depend on "yes" and "no". And similarly about the facts of "true" and "false", etc. Many issues, human issues, depend on these terms. All these terms are *multiordinal* as you will see later and they have different meaning on different levels of abstractions. Otherwise, I don't know what we are talking

Lecture Seven

about without indexes. 'Insanity' is merely maladjustment to 'facts' and 'reality', and again, 'fact' and 'reality' represent multiordinal terms.

You cannot say something about a 'fact' without regard to its *context* and there are as many 'facts' as there are contexts. Language can be elementalistic or non-elementalistic. That is a 'fact' *in this context*. Then we cannot treat 'facts' and avoid confusing them *without indexes*. We cannot hope to keep all these 'facts' clear without using all the extensional devices. This is how the self-reflexiveness comes in. Thus, we can talk *about* 'facts', *about* 'facts', *about* facts, and they are not *the same* without some regard to context. We must keep them straight. So, if we use the extensional devices we will automatically be on the safe side.

There is a good example of this in a question a friend asked me. He was a psychiatrist and, after seven years of working with him, he asked me a real question for the first time. He asked me,

"Do I 'copy' animals in my stomach reactions?"

"Do I copy animals in my nervous reactions?"

"Now, if you answer 'yes', it will make no sense to me."

That is what he asked me after seven years of work, and it is a good question. Now here is the question I want to ask you: Is that question he asked me *extensional* or *intensional*? *Intensional* because you *cannot separate stomach from the nervous reactions*. We have here only *one* definition of "copy" and by definition we have only *one* "copy". But how about the extensional facts, how many "copies" do we have extensionally? In this context, *two*. We abolish the difficulty then by indexes. We have then copy$_1$ and copy$_2$. And the problem does not exist any more. The problem is eliminated, just by indexes. Extensionally, they are *not the same* "copy". Investigate. If we would investigate we would find that we do not 'copy' animals in their stomach reactions, which if we did it would be desirable because we would have no 'nervous indigestion'. How about copying animals in their nervous reactions (copy$_2$)? That is not *the same* "copy". The extensional indexing of the intensional "copy" solves the problem.

If we have indexes, etc. (the extensional devices), in our heads we will not be confused. All of this applies to you, and everybody else.

Now I will show you a verbalistic scandal. The story about Achilles and the Tortoise, do you remember it? The Tortoise was a very slow animal and Achilles was very fast. Obviously Achilles can over-run the Tortoise. However, I will show you verbally that verbalistically and intensionally, the opposite should be *expected*. This is a verbalistic scandal 2,500 years old. This is called the "Paradox of Zeno", and you may be familiar with it. Achilles is put a little behind the Tortoise because he is so much faster than the tortoise. Now Achilles would have to halve the distance between him and the Tortoise before he could over-run it. Then he would have to halve that half, and then he would have to halve that half, and then halve that half, etc., and he would never over-run the Tortoise. Yet a child knows that extensionally it is not so. Such are the dangers of linguistic and semantic issues. The greatest men in the world have tried to solve this verbal paradox and have failed. You can see the dangers of that simple linguistic scandal, and in your life there are dangers just like this.

When you get a problem like that you can automatically solve it by extensional devices. The problem of sanity and 'insanity' for instance. The key problem there is the problem of adjustment to 'fact' and 'reality'. That is the main problem of psychiatry. Sanity and 'insanity' is only a problem of adjustment to 'fact' and 'reality'. Remember that.

In a psychiatric society of which I was a member there was an old lady, for thirty years a psychiatrist, who presented a paper which was quite inadequate. There was a younger brilliant psychiatrist who criticized the paper quite unkindly. That old psychiatrist burst into tears and cried out, "My God, I wish someone would tell me what a *fact* is, and what *reality* is."

What is the answer, if there is one? Remember, her question was what a "fact" and "reality" "is". The solution is that in the abstract, "fact" and "reality" have *no meaning*. "Fact" and "reality", being *multiordinal* terms have meaning only in a context and therefore with an index. This is a far-reaching subject. You will find all of that worked out in my book under the index heading of *Multiordinality*. The most important terms we have are multiordinal and have meaning only in a context. Now you may see why we must have indexes, and dates, etc.

I spoke about the boy who had no cortex but had a thalamus. Now a fish has no cortex but a thalamus. That fish is *adjusted*. It lives and swims around in the water. That boy was not adjusted though. Then 'thalamus$_1$' is not 'thalamus$_2$', etc. They have to be indexed too.

We are passing on tonight a little more into the problems of similarity of structure. We should investigate the facts of this world before we can talk more about similarity of structure. That is only reasonable. More than thirty years ago Rutherford produced an empirical *dynamic* process theory of 'matter'. Then came, ten years later, Bohr who presented us with an electronic theory of 'matter' in 1913. And since we went on, then came the so-called quantum theory of 'matter', and then in 1926 de Broglie and others produced the wave theory of 'matter' which has the acceptance of physics because it can predict facts that happen. So more than thirty years ago we lost the feeling of the so-called 'solid matter'. 'Matter' became a process of a swarm of electrons, a mad jazz of 'electrons', 'protons' and 'whatnot'.

I will not go into details of this electronic theory for the simple reason that the main point for us is not in the exact theory. The radical departure from the old is all that interests us here, and that is the dynamic character of 'matter'. Matter is supposed to be made up of a positive core of electricity (P) in the following diagram with negative electrons (E) running around it. They started with a circle for the path of these electrons but then went to an ellipse and now they have a wave theory, but this does not matter here. From a solid static 'matter' theory, we are passing to a dynamic process theory. This is the crucial departure from the old. In modern science what was negative becomes positive. It is *positive* that the negative results will remain;

namely, that the old is impossible and that what is the positive theory 1937 does not matter so much.

You are familiar with gold. Are you possibly familiar with quicksilver? Now they are different. They are chemically different. But the difference dynamically is just one less [proton]. The whole aspect chemically is changed by that one [proton]. So the altering of the dynamic structure changes the chemical structure and hence 'sense perception'. Suppose I have this table before me and I lean on it. It is solid. By the dynamic theory it is a table of electronic processes that supports me. It is made of moving electrons, but I don't go through it. The table by the solid theory and the dynamic theory are different. But the table is 'the same' for all practical purposes. However it is not the same table by static and dynamic theory. That is the great difference.

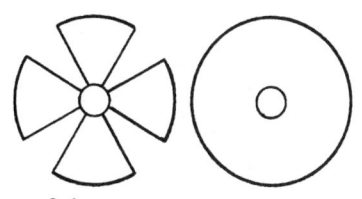

Here I have a fan with *four blades*, when I spin it you will see a disc. But there is no disc. This is what our nervous system does. All this is a fundamental fact. Not only of the world, but a fundamental fact of the nervous system (or the camera), that we see a disc where there is no disc but only rotating blades. By this you see the solidity of an object where there is no object, only rotating electronic processes. We see each other as 'discs', when we are only 'rotating blades' of electricity. This is what happens then. You and I, and everybody else, are only 'rotating blades'. You must be thoroughly convinced of that *process character of nature*. If you are not, look at one of your photographs of some years ago and you will be convinced that we are changing dynamic processes.

You can add to this process orientation iron, gold, and everything else. Everything turns out to be a dynamic process according to newest discoveries. Not much different from you and me except we are more complex than a piece of iron. It takes function and energy to be iron. Not much else.

We are still on the anthropomorphic 'objective' level, which is made up by the nervous system and does not exist independently in nature. That disc was only in our heads. So is everything else. What is outside your heads are only dynamic processes and *dynamic stimuli* which in our heads produce the 'object'. That table is no more solid than it is a dynamic process which I with my nervous system abstract, recognize, and react toward as I do. There is a book by Max Born, *The Restless Universe*. It is a very good book on this subject; you should all read it.

Here I want to show you some fundamental energies of nature. Before we approach that subject let me say that 'time' (I have just noticed we have little left tonight), 'time' is only in our heads. There is no 'time' in this world outside of us. We have clocks and you compare processes and processes, but there is no 'time'. There are only times with an 's' in nature. They are only summarized as beats, a summary of the vibrations in all of us.

When we come to *fundamental* questions there is no asking, "Why". There is no "why", that is the old stuff. Asking "why" is silly, both ways. When it comes to *fundamental* facts of nature, take things as granted. Here are two little balls of wood covered with aluminum paint. They are supposed to be non-electrically charged. As everything in this world is electrically charged, they have electricity, but it is neutralized. If we would test that as electricity we would find that is neutral, 'non-electrified'. Now here is a glass rod and I rub it on a fur. This fur has what is called positive electricity, and I electrify the rod by rubbing it on the fur. When I approach that positively charged rod to one of those balls, the neutral electricity in the ball will be divided, the negative will be attracted and the ball will be attracted to the rod. Then when I touch the rod to the ball and eliminate that negative electricity that was attracting the ball, the ball will remain positive and will jump away. You see, first attracted and then repulsed. Now those two balls are electrified, and this rod now repels the balls. The law is that *like* repels *like*. The ball is electrically positive and the glass rod is electrically positive so they repel. If we take a piece of hard rubber this produces a different kind of electricity again and this one will attract the positively charged balls. The other was finally repelling the two balls. Now those are fundamental energies in nature. Like electricity repels like and attracts unlike. Is that clearly understood? You have seen it in the way those two little balls were played with.

That is exactly what is going on in our nervous system. That is the importance of this. You have had sometimes a little drop on the end of your nose. Some form of energy was holding it. Before a drop of water from a faucet dropped, something was holding it together. We call that *surface energy*. No 'why' but just call names. We can measure that 'surface energy' by weighing the drop when it finally drops. We thus measure the energy that holds the drop together. This is, as a rule, small but it depends on the surface. If you will take a little pellet, say the size of a pea, and pulverize it you could make it so fine that it would cover half an acre of land. The surface would then be large, and if there is such an entity as *surface energy*, that surface energy of the pulverized pellet would be large. Well, if we had very small particles, extremely small, suspended in an appropriate medium, then interplays of energies begin and sooner or later life happens. The suspension of the little particles in an appropriate medium we call "colloidal" and the study of this leads to the theories of *colloids*.

Look at my smoke. It is made of very minute particles of carbon suspended in air. And clouds are particles of water suspended in the air. All of that are colloids. Any particles of something suspended in another medium are called colloidal. The separation between any two of these particles is of two kinds. Each particle is electrified with the same kind of electricity no matter what it is. They repel then each other. Now the surface energy attracts. These opposing energies are in the rough the whole of colloids. And so the colloids as particles are never at rest to begin with. They are never static; they have an interplay of repulsion and attraction, continually.

Now there is a drop of molten glass dropped into cold water. It is like a pear with a long tail. This is called Prince Rupert's "Tear Drop". (Demonstration.) When that molten glass congeals there are terrific surface energies developed. This equilibrium would last indefinitely by itself, but dynamically you can fancy it is just holding particles together. If you disturb nothing it will remain, but if you disturb and rip off one small part of the tail it will explode. By breaking off the little tail we disturb the equilibrium, the whole thing will explode, and *it is dangerous* for the eyes. *Do not play with those drops by yourself.* I will break one end of that tail, *you listen for the explosion and then I will show you the resulting powder.* I will do this within my hand to keep the glass from flying into our eyes.

The whole thing explodes just by breaking off one small part of the tail. You can see from this what surface energy means, what a powerful role it plays. And remember that all life is colloidal. That is a main point. We begin life with a very dispersed colloidal structure, and death is nothing but coagulation when the particles come finally together. And, all the time we are coagulating more and more. I do not say dying, but rather coagulating.

Now here is a white of an egg. (Demonstration.) You know, an ordinary white of an egg. If we add alcohol to it, it will coagulate. Try this yourself. When you add the alcohol you will see little strings form and then it begins to coagulate as a whole. It ends as a 'boiled egg'. I want you to visualize permanently these experiments. They are fundamental for the understanding of the colloids. We will go into this more later. These issues are fundamental; they include life, and remember your colloids are *affected* by *semantic and linguistic environments*. But we will go into this later.

SEMINAR LECTURE EIGHT

I was speaking about the structure of language and for the first time in history, we get the *examples* of what is meant by the structure of language. This has never been done before. This is where elementalistic and non-elementalistic structure and terms come in. And this is very important. From these our work here developed. We come to great dangers by identifying our feelings with our words which are not similar in structure to the facts. In some of my classes I prepare beforehand a demonstration with a girl student to have her drop a box of matches which I will hand her, and then I pretend to get mad at her and scold her and finally slap her face. All of this has been arranged beforehand with the student. Now out of a class of seventy about sixty-five will shiver at what I have done. But that is an illegitimate shiver. You do not realize the seriousness of what I am telling you. The people who shiver cannot delay their reaction; their 'judgment' involves immediate signal reflex reaction. Now the verbal explanation for my act may be this and that and many of them until finally it might be that the whole thing was a scientific experiment, which it was. Those people have no right to shiver and have animalistic signal, reflex reactions (intensional) — when there are so many possible explanations. They have jumped to conclusions immediately translated into organic reaction. The reaction is an explanation; they have gone beyond what they could see. This is very important. We know this 'jumping to conclusions', we might call it that. This is an *undelayed reaction*, which is animalistic. When we have a *delayed reaction* we have time to think it over and it will be legitimate. When you do orient yourself in terms of indexes, dates etc., you *automatically* have *delayed reactions*. What people have seen they have seen, but some of them will 'think' further. This is a *general reaction* and here *extensionalization* plays the most important role.

We start with maps, tables, and chairs, etc., but the importance of our premises is in dealing with, not chairs, but dealing with a delayed reaction. We try to prevent too quick 'judgment' translated without delay into an organic response, which as a rule is an unjustified reaction. Now the fellow who did not shiver but waited to see what happened next, had a balanced delayed reaction and saved himself from a painful and perhaps harmful shock. The non-shivering person then had delayed more balanced reactions which make for maximum happiness in life. This has application to general life. In my book *Science and Sanity* an attempt is made to investigate whether there are factors in science leading towards sanity and a better life or toward 'insanity'. I wish you would take problems of sanity and 'insanity' more seriously. There are very few people in this world who are perfectly adjusted to life. Their maladjustment is due mostly to intensional orientations and their progeny, definitely harmful intensional doctrines. To a large extent these dangers disappear with *general semantics*. The questions of maladjustments go by degrees. You will understand this better when I come back to the colloidal foundations of life.

There are degrees of maladjustment, about this class it could be said that it is nearly normal. But we are not entirely 'normal'. So to introduce better adjustment and balance in our daily, national and international lives, through our reactions, we need extensionalization. You will see how the colloids come in later tonight. When life begins to pile up on us, the more maladjusted we are the sooner we break down. Education should give us sanity, real education, based on the results science gives us. A good school should train us in those neuro-linguistic and neuro-semantic factors needed to make us better fitted for happier and saner living.

Here comes psychiatry. I speak about psychiatry for the simple reason that if anyone analyzes you here tonight, you are *supposedly* normal. But we are very complex; in any one of us we cannot observe the mechanisms working in comparative simplicity. When we deal with patients in psychiatry, we deal with simplified and sometimes isolated mechanisms. We separate that one from the rest and examine them, we can watch them working; in other words, we learn *structural* data on the working of some mechanisms, which results become general. Each of us has similar mechanisms as the 'insane', except that it is only a problem of degree. Psychiatry has advanced so much faster than 'psychology' because it deals with only one mechanism at a time.

There is one problem I would like to elaborate a little. That is infantilism. We may be grown up chronologically but our reactions may be like a child's. That is infantilism. That is, we evaluate like an infant. Look in your own life and the lives around you and see how some evaluations in adult people differ from infantile and how often they are similar. Suppose I scold someone for not making notes and he makes a fuss and breaks into tears. That is infantile. If infantilism is too marked, this may become dementia praecox. In dementia praecox there is infantilism going on colloidally in the organism. Dementia praecox is today such a menace to the United States that special national investigations are in progress to get at the cause of this dreaded disease. And all this is closely connected with infantilism. With infantilism goes various sexual troubles. Masturbation, homosexuality, impotency, frigidity, etc., factors that make marriage and life so very unhappy. If you marry such an infantile person you believe you are dealing with a responsible individual, and you have to deal with an irresponsible, often amoral infant. You do not have any predictability, life becomes one agony of uncertainty, worry, fear, what trick the infant will play, etc. Perhaps you begin to see the meaning of our work.

Of late psychiatry begins to pay more and more attention to 'the unconscious'. Humans differ from animals by the amount of their consciousness. This consciousness governs our lives. For instance, I had a very brilliant student, a university man, who went to a number of psychiatrists, was adjudged incurable, and who besides other disturbances had symptoms of 'epilepsy', loss of consciousness and whatnot. After I worked with him in my seminars conjointly with a psychiatrist who applies GS and whose patient he was, this student now is back in the university, supposedly well, or at least greatly improved. Here is the explanation the way I see it. Epilepsy is connected with a certain brain activity (epilepsy$_2$) and a certain disease of the brain (epilepsy$_1$). We know very little about it. But epilepsy$_1$ is connected with a certain disease of the brain most of the time, and this usually is incurable. Analyzing this fellow's 'epilepsy', though he had 'attacks', etc., he did not impress me that that epilepsy$_1$ was genuine, and I came to the belief that he did not have un-indexed 'epilepsy' because he had just 'attacks'. He did *not* lose consciousness, he was just over-absorbed. It was not loss of consciousness. It was over-absorption. Try this yourself. When you 'think' hard you get tense. Usually over-absorption is connected with a mild form of epilepsy as Doctor Rosett has shown (*Archives of Neurology and Psychiatry*, April, 1929). And in this case I utilized the data of Doctor Rosett, indexed 'epilepsy$_1$', 'epilepsy$_2$', etc., and told him that he was only over-absorbed and that it was not 'epilepsy$_1$' but 'epilepsy$_2$'. And it disappeared. The understanding, consciousness of the mechanisms, helped a difficulty, and it does so in nine cases out of ten.

Let me show you another example. The British started the so-called anthropology. They collected facts about primitives. The facts were correct enough, but their interpretations were not correct. They ascribed to those primitives they had found, low-grade white man characteristics. That is the same mistake as to consider an infant as a '*little man*'. You know an infant is not a little man but has characteristics of his own. You cannot then judge the primitives as imperfect white men. You must put the primitive on the primitive level and not judge him by white standards. The French and Polish school of anthropology corrected this error and put the primitive on the primitive level and we treat primitives today scientifically on their level, yet today we have not studied the white man on the *white man's level*. That is very complicated, but for the first time, in GS, we are treating white men on the white man's level, and this is based on consciousness of *abstracting* what is going on outside and inside our skins. When that 'epileptic' became conscious of the mechanism of his condition, his un-indexed 'epilepsy' disappeared. By placing the white man on the white man's level we base neuro-semantic and neuro-linguistic reactions on the similarity of structure, and so make them extensional, and this is the beginning of the solution, and then all known details connect together in a harmonious whole.

This is where mathematics comes in. The great mathematician, Sylvester, said "Mathematics discovers similarities among differences and differences among similarities." Think that over. This is very important. When we have only intensional definitional orientations we go by similarities neglecting differences. But the facts of life always include differences. Don't marry a definition or you will have to go to Reno. You will have to *live* with a man or woman Smith, not the definition, and differences from definitions become imperative. You have a 'chair', that is a label only for a definition by similarities. But if you have 'chair$_1$' you have similarities in the 'chair' (definition) and *differences made conscious by the index*. Old education fails because intensional teaching is done by similarities while each

Lecture Eight

individual is different. Watch please the way I lecture. I am conscious all the time of your *differences*. Do you see I watch you all the time? I am watching to see if you are responding properly to our progress. I don't want anybody to miss the points of advance as individuals. This *consciousness* of *differences* affects life and affects professions. You get very little out of the standard intensional attitude going by similarities. It does not work, except in the simplest cases.

I will tell you now how general coordination by extension comes in. I was on a sea voyage and in my stateroom there was a card table and a rickety chair. I had a guest who asked me what the structural differential was for. I explained, using the definition chair, and the actual chair$_1$, the *difference* between orientation by my definition of the 'chair' and the orientation by realities, chair$_1$. I was explaining that chair$_1$ to him and I picked it up to show him. When I picked it up the chair was so rickety it was falling apart, but I did not know this. And then I said that if I sit on the *intensional definition* and there is something wrong with the actual chair, I would collapse. Then I explained to him again, still shaking the chair, that I was a person with an extensional orientation and you ask me to have a seat, and I say to myself, and that means chair$_1$, chair$_2$, etc. So I shook that chair some more. I said, "I sit, then, not upon a definition 'chair' but on that individual chair$_1$ in my hand." And then I sat down with a great deal of energy on that chair, which was so rickety that it collapsed. My extensional chair$_1$ went all to pieces. But I did not fall down. Extensional orientation gave me coordination. You see this is what it means. I was something like five inches from the floor but I did not fall down. I was quite surprised myself, but the reason was that consciousness that we deal with a unique individual which you cannot trust blindly. We orient ourselves by definitions or by intension only. We trust blindly. I want to stress that by extension we are perfecting our *consciousness* by being *conscious* of dissimilarities or differences, as well as similarities.

Here comes the problem of *teachability*, what can be taught. Here, I am introducing differences as a fundamental yet neglected factor. Differences are factors in similarity of structure. It is, then, important to have a discipline that can teach us in general about differences. You cannot imagine anything more important than to train in similarity of structure including differences. In the old way we have no method of teaching and training in differences in general. I cannot *train* you in differences in general outside of a particular case when I show you the particular differences. But only in *particular* cases. In the old way we were helpless to train *generally* in differences. We can, however, train you generally in differences, and we can make you conscious of differences in general by the use of *extensional devices*. The old way trained in differences in particular cases but the new way trains generally, by extension and non-identity. Through this generality we pass from intension to extension. I know most of you are not aware of the extensional value of mathematical methods. Have you heard of Newton and Leibnitz? They both, independently of each other, produced the differential calculus. Very few mathematicians even realize that their greatest achievement was the formulation of a *general theory* in mathematics. Mathematicians for over two thousand years had differentiated and integrated in *particular instances*, but that was not *teachable*. That is the whole business. That is the whole difficulty. The fact is that we can show you the particular differentiation but we cannot teach it in general. Newton and Leibnitz made differentiation *teachable*. I want this to be clear. This is the historical value of general theories — they become teachable.

Life is made up of similarities and differences. Differences, in the meantime, are often much more important than the similarities. Take an example from life. If you take two people from here and marry them by definition they would not be happy, because they have individual differences not in the definition. You can see how important it is to have *general methods* for training for differences. This does not exist in intensional orientations but does exist in extensional orientations.

Neurosis and psychosis are often made when a father or mother hurts a child and because the child hates intensional "father", which is general, the child hates all fathers and becomes neurotic. But suppose he is extensionalized. I will add indexes to him. He will hate $Smith_1$, not all fathers and will not become a neurotic, etc. In a great many cases my students are very poorly adjusted to father and mother difficulties and I have told them to stop using the terms and call them $Smith_1$, etc. And in many cases these difficulties have been cleared up. This applies to "mother" too. "Mother" is an intensional term but extensionally the "mother" is only "the woman who has borne me or you". That is extensional. But you will not hate all "mothers" then, if you hate only the "woman who has borne me". This is the extensional view because the facts are that "she has borne you". The old intension hides the difficulty in the unconscious and this works havoc with us. But by extension we drive those hidden difficulties from the unconscious into the conscious, because we are conscious that facts are not only similar but different. I will still deal with that subject further in the next lecture.

I was telling you that we are adjusting our orientations to the sharp revolution and profound change in our world outlook that has been made in the last thirty-five years by the dynamic process character of 'matter' which I tried to explain to you before. I showed you that disc that was made up of rotating blades — it was really rotating blades, not a disc. That disc did not exist actually. Your nervous system manufactured it inside your heads. This applies to all 'matter'. All you *see* is a nervous construct that you have made up. It is a *process*. Anything you *see* is made up of rotating electrons. What you feel is not what you see. It turns out that anything we can see is only a stimulus to our nervous system and therefore the 'object' we see has 'reality' only within us, although the outside electronic image has independent reality. This is important because the older theories are untenable. It does not matter what the details of the new theories are, it only matters that the old theories are untenable. This is *positive knowledge*. And that is destined to change our orientation from the old *static intensional two-valued aristotelian orientations* to the non-aristotelian infinite-valued dynamic *process orientation*. This is very serious. We are racially going to pieces because we *live* by the findings of modern extensional science, but we keep in our heads intensional systems of primitive origin, non-similar to the outside world and our nervous system. Our orientations do not fit the things that we live by. This is new.

I want to explain that two-valued orientation. Take the first one. Either object B touches A or does not do so. This is a two-valued orientation. "Either-or", "yes or no", "good or bad", "love or hate" etc., it is all *two-valued*. It was formulated by Aristotle as the law of the 'excluded third'. A is B or not-B, it touches or it does not. We call that two-valued orientation. Notice the *two* values. A third is impossible by this verbal formulation, contradicted by life experience. If the dynamic process theory of 'matter' is correct, as it is, demonstrated by endless data, then these two objects, A and B, do not exist outside of your head. Always think of the disc example. You can see the parallel between the nervous construct of the discs and the two-valued orientation. This applies to all objects. What actually exists outside our heads are electronic processes, electrical structures, that change continually. So electricity turns out to be the 'building bricks' of the world and ourselves. Now if everything is a process, a radiating jazz of electrons (an infinite number), we cannot say that *process* C touches or does not touch *process* D. They would have an infinite number of degrees of touching. So you see we must pass from the aristotelian two-valued orientations to the non-aristotelian infinite-valued process orientations.

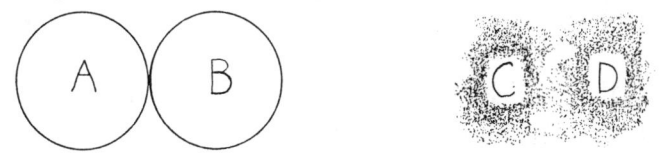

You all realize the importance in life of the motorcar, the aeroplane, and the radio. You are familiar with the names Euclid and Newton. Now electricity and the magneto will not follow the theories of Euclid and of Newton. Thus our *actual extensional lives* are lived under non-euclidean and non-newtonian conditions, our orientations remain, however, hopelessly inadequate as of the old. This applies to aristotelian two-valued orientations, with them we can arrange a dinner table, but cannot preserve *sanity — personal, national,* and *international*. Thus extensionalization represents a culturally necessary step from which there is no escape. Consciously we cannot go back, we can unconsciously. Consider the colloids. You must work on this "consciousness of abstracting". Do not forget that egg. Remember also those two little balls which were repelled when electrified, remember that surface energy demonstration. Now with these very small particles suspended in proper mediums with electrical energies repelling and surface energies attracting, when we upset the equilibrium of those energies things begin to happen. Remember the case of the egg. The secret of life depends on the flexibility of that proper dispersion or agglutination of those small particles in a proper medium which we know as living protoplasm. Take this box and this can. Why don't they come together? Because they are too big and there is no proper medium. When we swim it is the medium that makes the difference. In colloids the particles are very small and the medium is very heavy compared with those particles, therefore there is not a great deal of freedom for those particles to move about. This applies to protoplasm. We have colloids that are non-living too. Inorganic colloids, and you would be surprised to see what happens even in these. These can reproduce forms of life even when there is no life, only because they are made up of colloidal units which set up dynamic interplays of fundamental energies, as found in living protoplasm. On colloidal grounds very soon we will be able to produce artificial life. Now two particles with the sets of opposing energies make up a colloidal unit. When we interplay those colloidal units the *groups behave differently* than the colloidal *particles*, and we get *group actions* and reactions which although *unliving*, approximate the reactions of living protoplasm. Remember life is still more complex. Here I am only talking the simplest about those two energies, between only two particles.

But, when we come to cells, fibers, another important factor comes in. You know what polarity means. You see here we had only these two energies, but if we have a fiber made up of colloidal cells we have partitions and polarity and a plus electrical charge on one end, we have a minus electrical charge on the other end. An electrical current passing through the fiber will change the polarity of that fiber. And if you make a colloidal experiment and you have a lot of colloidal particles scattered about, then you pass an electric current they will go to opposite poles. This is the working polarity. Those cells are much more complex than I have said. This is very important.

And now can you see that if you are two-valued in your head you cannot 'think' about life where the facts are colloidal and infinite-valued? The common 'thinking' is two-valued but specialists even cannot 'think' colloidally if their orientation is not infinite-valued. Then life and facts are dynamic but language is static. With extensional devices and resulting infinite-valued vocabulary our language and orientations become fluid. Motion, however, is quite difficult. It goes by infinitesimal steps, but if we fix a date we get a static cross section of that process. The newtonian world was 3 plus 1 dimensional. Three for space and one for 'time'. We add motion. In four dimensions we also have motion although it becomes a static series of positions with a date. Otherwise, every point in space has a date. When you have a date affixed to a point, the point is then static. The world remains dynamic but the representation of facts now becomes static. In four dimensions every point has a date. A general assumption would be that electrons should be very similar. But in four dimensions everything is different because it has a date. We don't divide space and time at all. We have that space-time continuum with a hyphen. And in four dimensions everything is static, there is no motion but a static extensional series of events, yet physical 'motion' goes on as ever. So we cannot just say the world is dynamic and the language is static But we can adjust the representation to four dimensions and then we can represent the world as static too or language as dynamic. Thus the flexibility of our language can be used by extension. I want to cover another problem.

There is an instrument called the psycho-galvanometer. Experiments were made in hospitals and universities, mostly with students, using this machine to register self-generated electrical currents. They put the student in a chair and give him two wires to hold, and the wires are connected with the psycho-galvanometer. We produce our own electricity, and the psycho-galvanometer is a very delicate instrument. Any movement we make, 'mentally' or 'physically' is registered there. Other instruments register electrical currents in the brain and produce charts called encephalogram charts of brain waves Every different individual event in your life produces a different brain wave. Going back to the psycho-galvanometer, you hold two wires and I tell you something. You register what I say and report verbally and there is a curve traced in the psycho-galvanometer between our organic electrical and our verbal responses and it shows that our verbal responses are mostly falsifying the organic responses. There are a few terms that are very strongly registered. One term always registers very deeply with people, "Frustration". We know the horror of frustration. If we live in an intensional world one should expect frustration. When we speak, when we expect too much happiness, we are being frustrated by facts. We do not want frustration, so pass on to the new!

Remember our structure and function is colloidal, and colloidal structures are electrical structures. Otherwise, we are bunches of electricity. Every word, every action, etc., involves special electrical currents which we register organically as well as verbally. Every word changes our electrical currents, and those effect the coagulation or dispersion of the colloids. 'Think' about yourselves in terms of a colloidal jazz — colloidal jazzes that are going on in our brains. When we bring about a similarity of structure in my dynamic colloidal jazz and yours, then we understand each other. You can see now why people die from *words*. A dementia praecox has *over-dispersed colloids*. That is why it is so close to infantilism. Education is made possible by verbiage and electrical effects on the structure of the col-

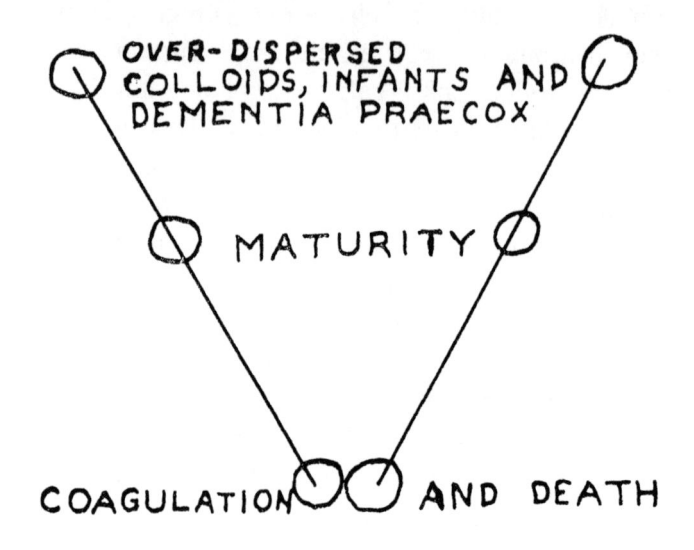

```
       OVER-DISPERSED
    O  COLLOIDS, INFANTS AND  O
       DEMENTIA PRAECOX
        \                   /
         \                 /
          \               /
           O  MATURITY  O
            \           /
             \         /
              \       /
               \     /
                \   /
                 \ /
   COAGULATION  OO  AND DEATH
```

loids. When you are born you have *dispersed* colloids. Death is coagulation. There is no need to call it anything more. Maturity is some stage in between these two.

SEMINAR LECTURE NINE

Thank you very much, Dr. Congdon*. It was a pleasure for us to have you here this evening.

In the U.S.A. the problems of infantilism and dementia praecox have become national problems and a menace. Research workers in thirteen scientific centers in various parts of the United States have been mobilized for the campaign to be launched by the National Committee for Mental Hygiene against dementia praecox, most prevalent of all 'mental' disorders. However, even these workers are ignorant of modern science and the neuro-linguistic and neuro-semantic issues involved. Their researches although useful, cannot be far-reaching enough, and remain, and will remain, paper-reports without broader applications. Studies and experience in General Semantics seem to throw new light on dementia praecox, adding the fundamental analysis of infantilism as a definite mechanism of maladjustment based on misevaluation, etc., etc., a preparatory ground for dementia praecox, formulated in workable terms.

---

* Before the seminar lecture, Dr. C. B. Congdon of the University of Chicago Health Service spoke on 'mental' health problems, with particular reference to schizophrenia. His remarks are not included here.

I will read you the latest definitions about dementia praecox, each one summarizing, so to say, empirical data of many observations, which entirely coincide with the observations we have made in General Semantics.

What is Dementia Praecox?

Definition by James V. May, Superintendent, Boston State Hospital

> Dementia praecox is a disorganization of the personality during the period of adolescence or maturity. It is characterized, in a general way, by an incoordination of the mental mechanisms and is associated sooner or later with an intellectual deterioration without any definite organic basis which can be demonstrated at this time.
>
> Psychologically, it is the reaction of an inadequate personality to the difficulties of environment. This inadequacy is not demonstrable in the intellectual field, but expresses itself in an inability to react, as the normal, well-balanced personality does, to the difficulties encountered during the course of educational, economic, sexual, emotional, domestic or social life of the individual.

Abstract from Textbook on *Clinical Psychiatry* by Dr. Edward A. Strecker and Dr. Franklin G. Ebaugh

> Dementia praecox, the mystery of psychiatry, constitutes a challenge to investigators in every field of medical research. Its etiology is unsettled; its pathology unknown and its clinical

limits in dispute and yet it is a more serious problem than either tuberculosis or carcinoma. There are twice as many hospital cases of dementia praecox as tuberculosis. Each year, not less than 30,000 to 40,000 individuals (including all cases), soon after adolescence or in the first flush of manhood and womanhood fall victims to this dread disease. Unless an adjustment is accomplished during the brief stage of incipiency, they are condemned to a veritable living death, devoid of emotional life and unable to participate in the normal activities and affairs of living. The importance of this group of psychoses from the public health (mental hygiene) viewpoint needs no further emphasis and preventive measures are of utmost importance.

Dementia praecox, often called schizophrenia, because it reveals a fundamental splitting between the emotional, the thought and the motor processes, is a chronic psychosis which has its greatest incidence in the second life decade. It is scarcely a clear-cut disease entity but a creation type — a maladaptation. In the vast majority of cases, the end state is one of deterioration which particularly involves the mood of affective responses.

Adolf Meyer made a constructive formulation when he described the so-called "shut-in" personality. The tendency to be seclusive and to withdraw from reality, usually manifested in childhood, is the distinctive characteristic of the personality on which dementia praecox is so readily engrafted.

Excerpt from an article on "Dementia Praecox, A Simplified Formulation" by Dr. R. G. Hoskins in the *Journal of the American Medical Association*, April 11, 1931.

Dementia praecox is a disorder that characteristically takes onset in the early prime of life and persists for many years. In terms of total economic loss it costs approximately a million dollars a day in the United States alone. Its cost in human misery cannot be calculated.

The disorder has been recognized in its main features from the dawn of medical history. Why, then, in this age of medical advancement, has understanding of its causation and treatment so woefully lagged? The important reason, no doubt, is sheer fatalism, an attitude thoroughly unworthy of twentieth century medicine. More important, and to a considerable extent growing out of this fatalistic attitude, is a large measure of simple neglect. So heavy is the burden of mere custodial care that only the scantiest resources have been made available for research in this field. Practically, an important reason for failure of progress is the lack of a formulation comprehensible to any but trained psychiatrists. To the ordinary practicing physician, to the families of the patients, and to the nurses and attendants in psychiatric hospitals, in whose hands the welfare of the patients mostly rests, the nature of the disorder is largely a mystery.

Concisely formulated, then, it can be said that dementia praecox is a defensive reaction in a sensitive human being to a feeling of personal failure. It results from inability to meet one's own personal standards. It is characteristically accompanied by a sense of isolation. It may take the form of panic, of despairing acceptance (loss of hope), of evasiveness, with projection and grandiose delusions, or of simple acceptance of inferiority. Fundamental to the psychosis is an intolerable loss of self-respect.

In much 'insanity' there is a partial rationality but this is not to be relied upon in most cases. There is a case of dementia praecox that I will not easily forget. This was of a young soldier. He was always a good soldier but he developed certain undesirable characteristics. He would walk right out of a parade and go to the barracks and go to sleep, etc. He was punished and court-martialed, but he developed so many of these odd habits that they finally sent him to St. Elizabeths Hospital for observation. I spent two hours with him and he acted perfectly 'normal' and yet he was really almost a corpse. A corpse has as much life as that fellow had. He had not a trace of affective response. You would have to see a person like that before you could get the feel of the absolute lack of feeling. And, three months later he was a complete wreck. Here is that lack of *feeling* that Dr. Congdon spoke of, the *"living death"* of textbook definitions.

Returning to the colloids, the colloidal background of life is completely established. I remember another patient, he had been in confinement for twenty years. He had ground parole and went for strolls around the lawn. I studied that man — he behaved quite well. We could say 'quite normal', in the hospital. Remember the quotes. And then after twenty years he was lucky enough to die. And, when they made an autopsy they found he had *no 'brain'* at all in the ordinary sense. The cavity was full of 'pus'. There was practically no 'brain' in the ordinary sense. Now, how can it happen that a person can react 'quite normal' under limited conditions, the limitations of an asylum? How can he live? Colloidally we can explain it on the basis that the organism reacts as a whole. The function of the nervous system, as well as the whole body, depends on the colloids. And, therefore, although physiologically, in the old way, it could be said that the man had no 'brain', colloidally that cavity was full, and this carried him through almost 'normal reactions'. Today we realize that we have to revise all our sciences, and utilize, frankly, extensional methods.

For instance, there is no colloidal-chemistry; it is all colloidal-physics. Today that revision is going on, but it is not yet complete nor coordinated. Do you realize that today our medicine is only glorified veterinary science because of medical ignorance of psychiatry? I know a lot about horses and they are quite like us organically; but then why do they have so few and such simple diseases? The answer is that neuro-colloidal factors, semantic environment, brain environment, linguistic environment, etc., affect our colloidal structure. The fraction of an inch of more cortex in a human being is not a satisfactory explanation. Often, major operations are performed when the patient is only sick in the head. This is because medicine men are either ignorant of, or disregard, psychiatry. Since the colloidal works of Burridge, the medical sciences must be revised, as their formulations are *not similar* in structure to the facts.

It is not enough to rest behind linguistic issues and language. We must *feel* it as direct orientations, evaluations, etc., just as Doctor Congdon said we must. I want to give you an example. For instance, we have four different "ises":

1) "Is" an auxiliary verb.
2) "Is" of existence.
3) "Is" of predication.
4) "Is" of identity.

Examples: The first would be, "It *is* raining." The second, "I *am*."[1] The third, "A rose *is* red." And lastly, the "is" of identity, "The rose *is* a flower." We have four entirely *different* "ises" and yet have only one word for them. That is why we make error after error. The "is" of *predication* on the 'sense' level and the "is" of *identity are always, invariably, false to fact*. When I say "the rose *is* red", the language is *not similar* to the facts, it falsifies facts. The 'red' is in our heads, in our nervous systems, and we said that the 'red' was in the rose. Don't you see a falsification — a false-to-fact statement? In the rose we find only electromagnetic vibrations, not 'redness'. This applies to all 'sense' perceptions. I say, "The rose *is* red." That is not correct. You cannot say the sugar 'is' sweet. It is all in our heads,

---

[1] Although "I am" frequently appears as an example of "the 'is' of existence", perhaps "There is a principle of law which states ..." would serve as a more useful example. [HJM]

remember, not in the rose or sugar. So when we say 'sweetness' 'is' in the sugar, that is false to fact.

How about the "is" of identity? "A rose *is* a flower." The characteristics of a flower are not 'identical' with the characteristics of rose$_1$. Then that statement is false to fact. That identification of four entirely different 'is's' leads to human tragedies. These last two uses are *always false to fact* on the 'sense' level, and without the extensional devices we have no way of telling them apart, for they are spelled the same way.

Here is a desk. You call it a "table" — (1) an electronic dance — a process, and then with our nervous systems, we (2) abstract the 'object' and call it a "table". Then we have some sort of a (3) photographic, direct impression on the brain through our eyes, and we call the picture of it a "table", and then we have (4) a linguistic issue, a definition, which we call a "table". Do you like to have your knowledge and life orientations based on such falsifications, etc.? When we are conscious of these dangers they disappear, because we are conscious of what is going on in them and in our organisms, which are responsive to stimuli. It is difficult to deal in this field with students, or patients. Many times people answer my questions, but their words have no feeling or meaning. They are parrot-like. There is nothing behind them, no instinctive, organic evaluation of the issues explained. Mere verbalization will not work when it does not affect our organic responses and evaluations, corresponding to the issues. In GS we deal with semantic reactions in connection with what we are saying.

We cannot know what "diseased" means until we know what "healthy" means. "Superficial snatches of

Lecture Nine

medical learning" are supposed to breed 'insanity'. Now let's see, extensionally. We 'know' a lot about ourselves, and we 'know' that we 'know' something. Then we find all that we 'know' really turns out to be false knowledge. That amounts to "snatches of medical learning". And it all happens to be false to fact. I will give you an example. Consider what we call the "sex glands". I don't use this name because it is a misnomer; I call them by their technical name, gonads. The name applies to male and female, and the gonads are internal secretion glands, say, 9/10 of the function of which is *vitalizing* the *whole* body, *the brain included*, and say, only 1/10 of their functioning deals with "sex proper". There are mechanisms that are called "hysterical mechanisms". They are based on our capacity of *projecting* some semantic reactions on any part of the body, organs, etc. You remember, for instance, we were speaking of physiological projection of color or pain. Thus, we projected the pain from the head to the finger when we pinched the finger. These projection mechanisms can be useful. They are survival mechanisms on the animal level. On the human level we may, however, get into difficulties because we have projection mechanisms which we call illusions, delusions, and hallucinations. These are present especially in all 'mental' illnesses. Therefore, an animal has no danger in using his projection mechanism, but a man has great danger because he can overwork the mechanisms and trouble begins. In hysterics, for instance, we can have false pregnancy with every symptom present but the baby. Now this applies to some animals, dogs, for instance. Otherwise, it shows that hysterical projection mechanisms are very fundamental mechanisms. We can have all kinds of diseases, all made by projection mechanisms. With these we must start clearing them up in our heads and then the symptoms disappear. Those mechanisms do exist as a fact, but at present we are using them mostly to our detriment. There is no reason why we should not use them constructively since they exist and we know they exist. And that is what we are coming to. There is a hysterical mechanism projecting Christ wounds on the hands. These wounds are called stigmata, and cannot be cured by ordinary medicine, but after *psychiatric treatment* the wounds disappear because colloidal mechanisms here are of an hysterical order. Those projections are general organic reactions, and are very powerful.

I was speaking about gonads, you remember, 9/10 of their functioning is vitalizing the whole body, the *brain included*, and only something like 1/10 of their functioning could be called "sex proper". Carrel says that if the gonads would secrete blue fluid the whole body would be blue, the brain very blue, and even the bones would be slightly blue. Now, "snatches of medical learning" *breed 'insanity'*. The same is true about *false knowledge*. We are directly aware of the 1/10 functioning of the gonads. But that is not necessarily correct because we 'know' it. Remember those quotation marks. I will repeat that. These facts help many of my students. It clears up many of their problems. We do not need to be told about this 1/10 because we are directly aware of it, but we *never know* about the 9/10 unless science tells us so. Otherwise, what happens is this: remember "snatches of medical learning" breed 'insanity'. Through 'false knowledge' we *evaluate* our 1/10 as 10/10 and that leads to endless difficulties. Now here is the sad part of it. If, through false knowledge, we evaluate the 1/10 as 10/10 and identify in value a small part of the functioning with the whole, and *project* the 9/10 of false knowledge on the 1/10 of which we are conscious, we disorganize both functions because this is based on false knowledge. Thus, humans must 'know' about the working of some of their organs *before* they can work properly. Is that clear? In connection with the projection mechanisms this is the reason why neuro-psychiatry must underlie all medicine. Many of these mechanisms are used in the old way only by hysterical, ill people, and in the old way we use many of these mechanisms destructively. With the elimination of false knowledge and consciousness of the mechanisms, they can be used constructively. In practice it works as predicted.

If we *project* the 9/10 on the 1/10, diverting *energy* from the brain, this projection of energy on the 1/10 results in overactivity. That is not a proper distribution of energy. The more we become conscious of these mechanisms, the more we are putting the white man on the white man's level. Remember my analysis of the thalamus and my explanation of how it gets over-stimulated. Now, the role of the cortex is to regulate and *protect* the thalamus. If we have our cortex full of *false knowledge*, our cortex is not working properly — instead of protecting, it stimulates the thalamus and the white race is deteriorating rapidly as a result of this. We need better neurological *control*, and there is no control except through the cortex. So, the training of the cortex in the new way is an absolute necessity. It is an absolute necessity for the sanity of the white race, curbing *sick* men such as different Hitlers, etc., who rule many millions of humans. Now how can we do this?

The cortex has many functions:

1) Dynamogenic effect. This means *generating energy*. Otherwise, the cortex energizes, ultimately, the whole organism.

2) Differential activation. This means some impulses can be counteracted by other impulses. In the old way we call that 'inhibition', but today we do not, or shouldn't, use that ecclesiastical and legal term in neurology. Then there are other things too.

We have to put an "etc." here also.

Now I will ask you a difficult question. If the nervous system works as-a-whole, are any of these aspects only *verbal fiction*? Can such separate *aspects* exist by themselves? The answer is *no*. All of them work together but there is one thing about the cortex that is *functional* and so not a *fiction*, that is, *delay of reactions*. This is the proper role of the cortex. It slows down the instinctive, *immediate reflex* reactions of the animal. Now the question is whether we can introduce *full conditionality* in the reactions of humans and to what extent human reactions could be made *fully conditional*. If we can stimulate the cortex we delay the reaction and we help the rest of the functions of the nervous system because it works as-a-whole. Unfortunately, very few people, even neuro-psychiatrists, realize this.

And, the point is, when we feel things, not merely linguistic reactions, but our inner, direct reactions, our inside orientations are affected. When you have trained yourselves to 'think' *exclusively* in terms of Smith$_1$, Smith$_2$, etc., we have automatically delayed our reactions. We will not 'blow' up.

You see, there are wisdoms in this, wisdoms which are so old. When you use the extensional devices you cannot help but have delayed reactions. And here we have mechanical means to stimulate the cortex, because we can *introduce delayed reactions automatically*. When I was explaining about order I told you that the term 'order' brought human sciences together with mathematical physics and then I said that through *order* we can directly stimulate the cortex. Now here I am showing you how that is done automatically.

It is a matter of *ordering the reactions*. By extension, we must *order* our reactions and introduce automatically delayed reactions. The main point is that which Dr. Congdon tried to convey, and which I also tried to convey. Remember I told you the word *table* covers, (1) the *process*, the electronic process which is invisible. It also covers, (2) the *object* table, as our nervous system abstracts or makes it. We have the one name "table" for (3), the *direct physical impression* on the brain, that is not verbal. We *call* it a "table". Otherwise, that word covers only our feeling towards it. We talk about our organismal reactions. We have also, (4) a verbal definition we call "table". You can imagine the difficulties of such a situation. By thinking in terms of extensional methods we do away with many artificial difficulties. Remember the use of extensional devices is not linguistic alone. We are interested more in our *direct reactions* within us. You must remember not only to listen to what I say, but try to visualize it. Get it inside of you. All of this comes automatically with the use of the extensional devices. Try to use them.

SEMINAR LECTURE TEN

As we are coming to the end of the seminars I must suggest that there are books that have to be owned and read. Yes, some books ought to be owned. Taking them out of the library is not enough. Those books have to be *played with* and studied and marked. And today with the pending revision of the structure of our language, there are only a few books that will not have to be revised. Do you realize that? You must remember that the white race is going on the rocks from the psychological point of view. The statistical prediction is that in 200 years there will be no sane white man left. We have to do something about this.

We cannot neglect those war clouds sick men like Hitler are producing. For, we will pay for those in blood and taxes. The sick Hitler went ahead because we 'the sane' kept aloof. But we all will pay for his 'mental' illness which swept a nation, through our own blindness. You never think about the next war. But, you should. We have to use our 'cosmic corns'.

Now, let me say something more about infantilism. We were talking about dementia praecox; remember that it merges with advanced infantilism. Advanced infantilism, or acute infantilism, may be considered the beginning of dementia praecox. Recall the colloidal dispersion diagram. In both of those conditions the nervous colloids are over-dispersed. And, this is why dementia praecox always has infantile characteristics and sometimes dementia praecox begins with marked manifestations of infantilism. This is why dementia praecox and infantilism became a national problem in the United States. There is some infantilism in all of us. So, the 'germ' of dementia praecox (infantilism) is within all of us, but in *different degrees*. But you must know this, because there is no other way of combating this condition without being *conscious of the mechanisms*. Then we can avoid the dangers. The consciousness of mechanisms is putting the white man on the white man's level. One of the characteristics of infantilism is self-centeredness. Self-love, not selfishness. This is the pathetic side. The world does not exist for you alone, and so self-centeredness can never be healthy. In some case to treat such a self-centered person, we must train him in "wise (social) selfishness". So I introduce the term, "*wisely selfish*" against the self-centeredness.

Let me tell you a story. At a dinner being given for me in New York there was an Englishman who was quite a paranoid type. And he "knew everything", and told me how stupid it is for me to care for anything, etc. He threw at me the Anglo-Saxon theory of *selfishness*. Oh yes, historically there is one, and I listened to all this, and finally I told him, "If you want me to be *selfish, I am selfish*. I am working as hard as I do, because out of selfishness I don't want to live in a world made up of men *like you*."

You see how verbalism can be switched and made appear to lead anywhere. This is a part of the extensional and so necessary departure from intensionalism. The

Lecture Ten   145

infant is self-centered. You can *watch* this in life. So are people acting like infants. Women who pass their sex around as the infant does a priceless diamond which you might hand him; they are infants too. *Low evaluation.* You have to know that. Our grandmothers called a prostitute 'over-sexed' but the majority of prostitutes have *no sex at all.* They are infants, who can be tickled, but they are *not women* with biological urges for propagation, etc. That is why they give themselves away. And *women* who have 'sex' and are forced into prostitution by economic or other reasons, seldom remain in this field. That is important. Those that do remain are infantile, and they are wrecked in a very few years.

I am using the term or rather the expression, "semantic age". It means the method of evaluation of a given age. I was training the staff of a school and I had also a *joint* class of girls age 13, 14, 15, and a class of girls age 15, 16, 17, all together. I gave them a course in General Semantics and as an accredited course. Then came examinations. I am showing you what *age does.* I lectured on a *younger level* for this joint class. In examinations I judged a paper on merits. I did not know who wrote it. It turned out that all the Senior girls had an "A" and all the Juniors a "B" without exception. The age had shown itself clear-cut. The Juniors "B" and the Seniors "A".

Now you know what a chronometer is. It is a very precious watch used by astronomers and in astronomical observations. Now you give that chronometer to a three-year-old infant and he will take that and begin to crack nuts with it. Now fancy that you are trying to *explain* it to the child. You will not succeed. The child would have no proper evaluation. But your evaluation is adequate because you know the value of the chronometer. Speaking about infantilism, you can see what semantic age or evaluation standard *means*. You know we try to speed you up to your own age, all the time. "Be your age." That is a good standard expression, put into practice in General Semantics.

You know the standard evaluating reactions of a girl when she is semantically, say 12. You must evaluate at *your age* for you are not little girls. You have to think about this. This is very important for family relations. Remember what happens. You have some family, 'father', 'mother', etc. If you are, say 22 chronologically, you are a young 'mature woman' according to chronological standards. Yes, but if you are 12 or 13 by *evaluational standards*, your 'mother' is probably trembling about you. You should know what you are doing. You should know better than a little girl of 12. But if your standard of evaluation is 12 and your age is really 22, you cannot be trusted, you can not trust yourself. Otherwise, if you are of age, if you are a mature woman, you should know what you are doing. Mother will not fret about you then. That is the point. A great many difficulties are eliminated by this. In my seminars I try to speed people up to their own age.

This is a correct statement. You understand now the question of self-centeredness of the infant. Remember we differentiate between self-centeredness and 'wisely selfish'. Remember that to be happy you have to live in a happy world. That is being wisely selfish to try to make this world as happy as you can. Look over your friends and see to what extent you will spot that self-centeredness. Take an infant. Here comes the question of *duration* of a feeling. Being capable of feeling something, of having a feeling. Suppose a child was told not to play ball in a room but the child did it just the same and broke a priceless vase. And then 'mother' comes and draws the child's attention and tries to scold the child. She is heartbroken because the infant's play has broken a priceless vase. And the child will cry and be "oh so sorry". But, five minutes later it is all forgotten, because the child has *no evaluation* of the damage it has done. He is infantile. And chronologically grown-up infants are the same. They will ruin a life, never realizing this.

Grown-up infants do irreparable harm to each other and they are "oh so sorry" for 15 minutes, but in the next five minutes it is all forgotten. In marriage there is nothing more unhappy than to be tied up with such an infant. Standards of evaluation come in, duration of affects, etc. Animals have very short duration of impressions. Infants slightly more, but grown ups should have lasting affects, etc. The worst and incurable dementia praecox cases are those which have no affect or evaluation at all. Many dementia praecox's joys and sorrows are of few minutes' duration. They leave us unaffected, because they are so shallow and infantile. And this applies to us. If we are supposed to be 'normal', quotation marks, and we do some harm, that should not be forgotten the next minute. The lack of affect, lack of feeling, is where the horror comes in.

I have to tell you, finally, that if you do not work hard for weeks and months you will never get the main benefits from General Semantics. It is not so easy. I make it simple and it is simple, but it takes an entirely new type of extensional reactions, which can be acquired only by hard work.

I will not repeat tonight. You are more or less at home with the points we have covered. Remember the four "ises". Remember the "is" of *predication* and the "is" of *identity* are by extension invariably false to fact. Remember that the facts are important. If you say the stick is black, this statement is false to fact. "The stick looks black to me", is correct. The facts are not changed, but the implications are different. That is the important thing about it. The first statement involves false informations, the second does not. When we use these "ises" we classify our evaluations inwardly. *It involves* an organic response. Then we identify something actual with a fiction and we live, then, in a delusional world. This leads to maladjustment. This applies to other words too, say "apple". This name applies to (1) the electrochemical process going on there; (2) it applies to the 'object'; (3) it applies to the impressions on our brain; and (4) finally to a definition. This one word covers four different things. That is not healthy. We cannot deal with such a situation. Never forget this. Remember that all 'sense' impressions are *anthropomorphic*. In the old way we are full of false knowledge. All I tell you here is old 'wisdom' but could never be applied by intension. People who want to solve their own problems must study extensional methods. I am only outlining the course here deductively; however, you must go to *inductive* sources as outlined in *Science and Sanity*.

Remember the amoeba. It responded to the prey that swam near it, because that prey produced bubbles of gases that had direct chemical effects on the amoeba. If we reproduce artificially the bubbles of gas near the amoeba, it will go through the same reactions and try to catch the bubbles of gas. This is not a 'wise' reaction from a human point of view. That bubble had no food value to the amoeba. That was a physico-chemical reaction. Watch that animalistic type of reactions. You will see yourself doing similarly every day. From a human point of view that shows poor evaluation. We are speaking about the organismal reactions of the amoeba, and we will use the term "identification". We could say about those artificial experiments that the organism of the amoeba *identified* and *evaluated* a bubble as food. This was an inappropriate evaluation.

As there is no identity in this world, although there is equality, equivalence, etc.; with any identification (when the amoeba organismally identified food with the bubble), proper evaluation becomes impossible. When we have *identifications* 'in value' of anything with anything, with humans it is often harmful or sick. On the level of the amoeba it is 'natural', on the human level it is often the cause of 'insanity' and other human difficulties. Identification in value in a world of non-identity cannot lead to proper adjustment as we cannot have proper evaluation. Identification of food and the bubble is not proper evaluation. Remember these terms are technical. Being technical, do not translate these terms or you will get into difficulties. It is just like in science, abolish the technical terms and you have abolished a science.

Now let's go to dogs, organisms that are much higher (more complex) than the amoeba. You are probably familiar with Pavlov's experiments that are being done about establishing signal reactions in dogs and collecting saliva, etc. In this way conditioned reflexes are built up and studied. There is a good book on this by Pavlov himself. Well, in brief, in the experiments they ring a bell, then the dog is given some food, and this is repeated many times. After a number of such experiences, when the bell rings, saliva appears whether there is food or not. This is called a *conditioned reflex*.

Here I want to draw your attention to a very serious linguistic tragedy, a scientific and human tragedy. You will see later that the reactions of dogs and men differ in *degrees of conditionality*. I am speaking here about the English, remember. If you call such a condition*al* reaction condition*ed* that "condition*ed* reaction" does not allow degrees of condition*ality*. But if you call it condition*al* that "condition*al* reaction" allows for *degrees of conditionality*. This is the tragedy. In condition*ed* we have *no degrees*; we cannot distinguish between human and animal reactions. Pavlov called these reactions in his dogs *signal reactions*. Pavlov in Russian has *signal* and *conditional* reactions. In condition*ed* there are no degrees possible. The term "condition*ed*" eliminates degrees of condition*ality*.* Thus, dogs' reactions are identified with man's and our whole work in GS is made impossible. Human reactions must have a high degree, or rather, full, infinite-valued conditionality, and we should have *symbol* reactions of evaluation, not signal reactions like dogs. All I am try-

---

* Editor's note: See *Experimental Basis for Neurotic Behavior* by W. H. Gantt, p. xvi, for explanation of shift from conditional to conditioned. (Paul B. Hoeber, Inc., New York, 1944.)

ing to do is to train you in full conditionality of your semantic reactions and make you distinguish between signal and symbol reactions.

Well, going back to dogs. From a human point of view that signal evaluation of the dog, when he secreted saliva for the bell and no food was not a proper evaluation. The dog *organismally identified like the amoeba*. And, the bell is not food. Let's go a little further. We humans should not identify a bell or the sight of something with food, etc., that would not be a proper symbolic evaluation. You know what little boys do to street cornet players. They chew lemons before the cornet players, who secrete so much saliva in their mouths that they cannot play their instruments. That saliva is not necessary. That reaction is not human, of too low degree of conditionality, an animal *signal* reaction, not a human *symbol* reaction.

Adjustment and *evaluation*, more than reflex organic response — that is what we need. Now let me give you another example of identification in connection with 'insanity'. A patient of Dr. Prince was 'mentally' ill and had also hay fever. Once Prince flashed from behind a screen to the patient *paper roses* and the patient produced all the symptoms of hay fever. The organism of the 'insane' identified the *sight* of the paper roses with the physico-chemical effect of roses, because they looked alike. There was no physico-chemical reason for organic symptoms of hay fever, except organismal identifications, poor evaluations, signal reactions, etc. These facts may convey to you the great *difference* between *signal* and *symbol* reactions. Animal *signal* reactions involve organismal identifications and so lack of evaluation. Human *symbol* reactions depend on evaluation, not animal reflexes. The difference is in the *delay* in reactions where our cortex may enter and work. And by extensional training in delayed reactions we train the cortex, and when we train in extension, we automatically train in delayed reactions. This is very slow. We must work at it. Work with ourselves. With GS we can add to life values, because it is the science of values in life. Pavlov spoke of the necessity for gradualness and gradualness in the accumulation of knowledge. And he also said we must go by facts for the basis of our knowledge. And he went further and said we must have facts as the basis in everything we know at all. Modesty was another requirement. And we must be 'passionate' in our work.

I was speaking about the building of a 'science of man' and putting the study and treatment of the 'white man' on the white level, something which has never been done before.

General Semantics because of extensional (physico-mathematical) methods accomplishes this, requiring a complete revision of existing doctrines. The above formulates a genuine challenge which modern science has to meet, to prevent the nervous degeneration of the white race, of which Carrel warns.

To what extent this indictment is justified may be illustrated by endless quotations from practically all existing 'scientific' literature, but here I will quote only an authoritative statement by two specialists. "The quality of responding to the signals, signs or symbols ... may be looked on as the unique expression of the highest type of integrative function. This quality, termed 'signalization' (Pavlov) OR 'symbolization' (A. Meyer), is the common denominator of all *conditioned* responses, which may differ enormously, etc." [*Archives of Neurology and Psychiatry*, May 1935, p. 1033.]

The empirical effectiveness of General Semantics depends, among others, on the *amplification* of the Pavlov *animal* reflexology to the *human* level by introducing "degrees of conditionality" (see *Science and Sanity*, pp. 328, 332-343) as yet noticed only by *one* psychiatric reviewer in the *Archivio Generale di Neurologia Psichiatria e Psicoanalisi*, No. 1 and 2, Vol. XVI, 1935. Obviously 'condition*ed*' reactions gives an incorrect and misleading terminology because: (1) Every reaction is condition*ed* by something, and (2) 'condition*ed*' reactions *cannot have degrees*, essential for the discrimination between animal and human reactions, and to a large extent between 'sane' and pathological human reactions.

In GS we deal with absolute individuals, Smith$_1$, Smith$_2$, etc., and we must sharply discriminate between animal 'signal' reflex reactions, of *low* degree conditionality, and human 'symbol' reactions which involve 'meaning', *evaluation*, etc., of potential *full*, infinite-valued *conditionality*.

The 'mentally' ill patient of Prince who had hay fever and *produced* an attack at the sight of *paper roses* (*Science and Sanity*, p. 128) illustrates both these points: (1) The *low degree* of conditionality of his reactions, and (2) the animalistic, reflex or humanly ill 'signal reactions,' at the *sight* of paper roses.

Thus even in 1935 in serious papers, 'symbols' were ascribed to dogs, and Smith$_n$'s reactions were read into dogs, and the dog's 'signal' reactions were read into Smith$_n$. In fact if we accept the terms 'condition*ed*' and 'signal' *OR* 'symbol,' we make it impossible to treat Smith$_n$ on the white man's level. The term 'condition*ed*' prevents the considerations of *degrees of conditionality* so characteristic of *human sane* reactions.

Such identification ("OR") of "signal" with "symbol" reads human reactions into dogs, helping also to read animal reactions into human reactions, and successfully prevents the discrimination between 'sanity' and 'insanity', and the treatment of humans on the human level. The animal reflexologist, through similar 'confusion of tongues', and making the degrees of conditionality impossible, reads the reactions of dogs into humans, making also the treatment of humans as humans, and a theory of sanity impossible. Other examples are abundant everywhere.*

---

* Abstract from "Neuro-Semantic and Neuro-Linguistic Mechanisms of Extensionalization" by Alfred Korzybski (*American Journal of Psychiatry*, Vol. 93, No. 1, July 1936).

SEMINAR LECTURE ELEVEN

I have just come back from Chicago, and I have very happy news in the sense that those fellows who do work on their own problems get benefits from our work. If *they* have worked, General Semantics has worked.

Doctors' reports are also unbelievably cheerful. I have had students, and doctors have had patients, men and women who were supposedly complete wrecks but the methods of GS worked. I do not know how I can impress you that there is only one way of getting hold of *sanity*, in the '*white world*', that is by getting *conscious of the mechanisms*. There is no other way. And the moment we have summarized mechanisms of sanity, gotten consciously hold of them, we should have the whole thing in hand. And at present, in 1937, there is no other method. We do not often need psychiatry, if we know the *factors of sanity*. At present you are mostly youngsters, quite free and care free. That will not remain this way through life. New responsibilities will come down upon you. You will have to meet them. But if you meet life in a way where you are *conscious* of the issues involved, and take care of them, then adjustment will be the reward. If you do not know how to handle life, you will have a mess, not happiness in your life. That is not idle verbalism. That is a statistical summary of happenings in the life of many humans. You cannot handle a situation if you do not know *how* to handle it. Investigate 'facts'. There is nothing to believe or not to believe here. *Investigate*.

If you will not investigate 'facts' you will not be adjusted to 'facts'. Considering the similarity of structure between the territory and the map, we must know something about the territory and map-making. If you are to know something about yourselves you must know something about your biological, physiological, neurological structure, etc. You are not taught these things in school at present as factors of sanity, neither are you shown how to apply the knowledge gained. You must be. Remember the aim of education is not to cram you with 'facts' which are meaningless to you. In the short period of a college education the students, however, can and should get a great amount of scientific method, not the technique of 'facts' alone. This technique alone, as applied in a scientific laboratory, will not carry them through life, *but the method will*. The whole of GS depends on modern scientific *method*, not specific technique, although it develops a technique of its own. Although in science the positive theories may not be secure, the negative results of the new are *positive*, that is, showing that the old is impossible, false to facts, worthless, etc. You cannot expect to adjust yourselves to modern life which is actually shaped by physico-mathematical sciences, if you do not happen to know anything about the dynamic structure of the world, or the *colloidal* structure of yourselves, etc. You cannot expect to know anything about anything if you do not know that much, or rather that little. We cannot manage ourselves and our lives in a world that is entirely different from our creeds. We cannot manage our lives if we know nothing about ourselves. The testament of a donkey would be: "Never do differently than your parents did. What was good enough for the old ass is good enough for a young ass." For humans it should be: "*Never do* as your parents did. Do it better."

Are we living in a donkey age or in a modern human age? You cannot as college people afford to be outside of civilization. The 'knowledge' of 'facts' you have will not help you if you are ignorant or twisted about method. We cannot keep donkey standards and still be adjusted humans. We cannot advance science if we retain infants' and donkeys' creeds. Education should aim to transform infants into adult, adjusted human beings. As you will do your own living in life, it is worth working for a while to get the benefits of the newer methods and extensionalization.

There is a fundamental difference between the new and the old that should be stressed. What we *see* about this 'stick' I am holding up is only in our heads. In my hands I am holding an electronic *process* which acts only as a stimulus to our nervous system, remaining useful in other ways. What we *see* is an outside fiction, 'real' only inside our heads. What I have in my hands represents a *process* the details of which we do not see. The human tragedy today is that we have endless knowledge but we never apply that knowledge because the new knowledge cannot be applied by the old two-valued intensional orientations. This is the horror of the whole thing and the educators should know that. We know a great deal but we *never apply* this.

Realize that all I say is elementary standard knowledge, but *never applied*.

In GS we apply what we know. The knowledge which I am trying to convey to you is not new, it is standard and elementary. But, I am trying to show you how to apply what we know. The aim of education is not to produce a mere technician out of you, but to produce a happy adjusted human adult being. You should be taught to apply the knowledge you have. There is not much use in teaching physics, mathematics, etc., if there is no application, no *human* application. The *infantile*, ultimately anti-social old slogan, "science for science's sake" is not valid any longer. If we teach scientific methods, then we can manage the rest by ourselves. We do not need techniques alone, but scientific methods are very important to us because we can apply the methods anywhere. This applies to the whole future program of education. Method, method, method, is much more important than a technique. In some isolated instances we need a technique, but that is not the whole thing. What I am stressing here is a summary of scientific physico-mathematical *method*, to be applied to life and living.

I am passing tonight to a most important problem which I call the *Natural Order of Evaluation*. If we want it or not we are living in this world and we have to adjust ourselves to this world or perish. Just because we live *in it*. The water at Olivet has iron in it. Whether you like it or not you adjust yourself to it. I have to have sandwiches once in a while, and I have to adjust myself when I find that the young fellow who is supposed to bring them to me has gone away to pa and ma and I get no luncheon. That is exactly the art of living, adjusting

Lecture Eleven

yourselves. This applies to all of us here. The art of living. Adjust yourself to the circumstances no matter if you are hungry. Here is a fellow who is supposed give me my luncheon, he is busy, or forgets it, or goes out of town. I am hungry. In the meantime, it is a situation to be met. There is no reason why I should have ugly feelings for that poor devil, if he has to go out of town and he does not tell somebody else to give me a sandwich. Remember I am very serious. This is an actual example. The fact is that sometimes he neglects me, that I actually am hungry, but I have no resentment because of my evaluation. I understand he has to go out of town. Evaluation involves understanding of a situation and you can tighten the belt on your stomach. Our stomach is not everything. There are other kinds of evaluations besides our stomachs. The question of food and comfort, etc., are not as important as the problems of evaluation in general. In this country they pay more attention to physical comforts than any other kind of evaluation. This is quite tragic. There is no human 'happiness' involved in that. On the old Continent we may starve, we may have many discomforts, but we are 'happier' than you are here with full stomachs, etc., and, if you want to make better progress here you have to pay less attention to your stomachs, baths, etc., and more to general evaluation of human time-binding, interrelationships. Starvation is not the worst thing we can get into. On the human level there are worse troubles than that. That is the question of education, *culture*, and civilization. There are worse troubles than mere starvation. In GS we take them into consideration.

Now, this stick represents only an electronic process. The process acts as a stimulus to our nervous system. This process character is very important. We do not see this process, our eyes *abstract* only this 'disk' from the 'rotating blades'. You see a disk where there is *no disk*. This *seen* cane represents also only a physiological abstraction. This is a fundamental of life, that life is abstracting from environment facts. It makes no difference for my walking, whether the cane is made up of an electronic dance with some permanence, or some invariance of function, or a 'solid object'. This process character is what we call today 'reality' given by science. And this is 40 years old, but never utilized as a type of orientation; impossible under two-valued conditions. In the meantime, this means a complete departure from the old and requires an infinite-valued orientation. The old 'objective' attitude is not correct. You cannot depend on what you see. It is not 'real', quotation marks. What then 'is real'? The term 'real' is a terrific term. The 'reality' of 'reality', try to get the English of it. Do not forget that in every one of us in this room and those who are absent, there are certain mechanisms working and we have to know the rudiments of physiology before they begin to work properly. The whole of psychiatry is based on the adjustment to 'facts', adjustment to 'reality'. And so, if we cannot solve the problems of 'fact' and 'reality', we are nowhere. As a white race, as a sane race, we are nowhere if we cannot get hold of the meaning of 'reality' or a 'fact'. And the whole of psychiatry, the whole of sanity *depends* on adjustment to 'facts', and we have to investigate how we can possibly find 'facts' and 'reality'. Remember the story of that old woman psychiatrist who cried: "What is a fact?" "What is reality?" Well, you will know it and you will not cry over such conditions for you will realize the difficulties of 'facts' and 'realities', yet it is manageable if understood.

I am passing now to the natural order of evaluation; this is the crucial point in GS, and I want you to get it thoroughly. Every one in this room has a definite evaluation, say, about the lectures. That evaluation is often personal. But we also must be impersonal and have to look centuries ahead. Just for example, say I ask one student what he thinks about the lectures and he says, "Oh, that whole study is worthless." Another fellow, though, will say the work is important. Here we have different opinions. One said under certain conditions one thing, and another said the opposite. Now, which is correct, and what will verify the opinion? Here we have a living human being, delivering a series of lectures to you, the opinions are "good" and "bad". Who will be the final judge, and the question is, what *human value* has my work. The empirical results and history shall decide, and here you will see how personal opinions do not matter. History will judge it by empirical results. Our private opinions do not matter. Now I dealt here in a problem of evaluation.

We must then, go to racial evaluation. We must consider racial evaluation — which we call "science" — not personal. You may like it or you may not like it, but it makes no difference. History will show whether a theory is valuable or worthless. In science we judge by prediction verified by facts. And this method is constructive, although the results are not final. There is *no finality*; and that is *final* (different orders of abstractions). Never say "never" and also never say "always". The final 'finality' is that there is *no* 'finality', because in life as we know it, things happen as against every kind of predictability. Maximum predictability cannot follow the old two-valued certainty, but must follow maximum probability.

I introduce you now to a new form of evaluation. There are problems of evaluation which are fundamental in our education, what I call the *natural order of evaluation*. This is the crux of the whole of GS and extensionalization. Those who are really interested in GS will have to study a great deal, and train themselves. Then GS will work.

I will speak now about relations. There are many kinds of relations, and it is a point where mathematics and logic come closely together. We will deal only with one particular kind most important for our purpose. Take the relation of [siblings].

Now, if A is a [sibling] of B, then B is a [sibling] of A. These kinds of relations are called *symmetrical* relations. Just because if A is the [sibling] of B, B is the [sibling] of A; otherwise it is reversible. Another type of relations, if A is the father of B, B is never the father of A. Otherwise, the relation is not reversible. That type of relation is called *asymmetrical*. A symmetrical relation can be reversed; but an asymmetrical one cannot be reversed. I am going ahead very slowly because this is a crucial problem. I have two girls here in front of me. Girl one understands *more* about, say, drumming than girl two. That relation is not reversible. An asymmetrical relation then. Mathematical relationships will mostly be asymmetrical. They are based on *more or less*. If A is *more* than B, or if B is *less* than A, B can never be more than A. This applies to all asymmetrical relations. All the relations based on "more" or "less" are asymmetrical by definition. They are then not reversible. A *symmetrical* relationship is reversible. When you are *evaluating* you are interplaying *asymmetrical* relations of "more" or "less". This is why asymmetrical relations are so important, because they are at the base of every evaluation and they are irreversible.

I hardly can tell you how important it is that asymmetrical relations are irreversible and all *evaluation* depends on asymmetrical relations, for if you like A *more* than B, you can *not* like B more than A. Hence evaluation depends on asymmetrical relations, and are irreversible. One of the serious tragedies of mankind depends on the fact that we have *reversed the natural order of evaluation.*

Our problem in GS is to return to a *natural order of evaluation* as shown by modern science. You have seen those little lumps of white stuff that is supposed to make coffee sweet. It is not sugar, and it has no food value. It has white coloring, it gives sweetness, but yet has no food value. That is not sugar. You have seen an apple, but the apple *you see* is only in your head, in your nervous system. You must index, date, etc., the apple because the apple a month from now may be rotten. This is where indexes and dates come in. Fancy I could produce an *artificial 'apple'* that would look, taste, and smell like an apple and yet not be an apple. Now, you are hungry and I give you that *artificial* 'apple' which will correspond completely to your *definition* of an apple, but your stomach does not want that 'apple'. It wants the physico-chemical process that is a 'real' apple. Remember, your stomach not your seeing or smelling. That artificial 'apple' would not satisfy your stomach. It wants *process* not the *abstracted* 'object'. In the natural order of evaluation then, the physico-chemical process is more important than the object abstracted by our nervous system. The *process* is more important than the so-called 'object'. Otherwise, what we have abstracted by our 'senses' *is not* what we need or want. We want and need food, etc., not something which looks like sugar, etc.

I spoke about an apple because it is more spectacular, but this analysis is entirely general, and applies to anything. The natural order of evaluation becomes clear, what we actually need is the physico-chemical *process* not the *nervous abstractions* which we call the 'object'. What you *see* as an 'apple' applies only to 'object'. It is 'sense perception' only, not the 'reality' outside our skin. Even if you are in love with somebody; what matters is not the object-fellow, not the 'human' as we *see* him, but it is the living process which is important. In general, the physico-chemical processes are more important than the so-called objects.

Processes as well as evaluation involve asymmetrical relations.

We have established one step in the hierarchy of *natural order*. The *event*, the electronic dance, or

Lecture Eleven

the physico-chemical process is more important than the nervous abstraction which we have made by abstracting, summarizing, etc., and neurologically building up the object. Never forget that.

Now, taking life as it comes. You are hungry; you want an apple. I may deceive you with a synthetic 'apple', but it will not satisfy your hunger. Thus, the process is more important than the object. Now I begin to speak to you *about* the *object apple*. That will not satisfy your hunger. Then: 2) the object is more important than words. We have said the process is *more important* than the object, now remember, an evaluation is an asymmetrical relation all the time. What is *more important* if you are hungry, the object apple or the definition? Try it if you are not convinced.

Do you understand the difference between descriptions and inferences? From descriptions we are drawing conclusions which we call inferences. I want to convey to you that 3) a description is *more important* than an inference. And if from inferences of lower order we pass to higher order inferences and so on, every lower order inference is closer to facts than the higher order of inferences. The lower order is closer to facts than the higher order inference. Otherwise, 4) the lower order inference is more important, or reliable than the higher order inference.

So we have here an exact *natural order of evaluation* which, for the first time, can be conveyed with the aid of the Structural Differential by all available 'sense' organs, thus the ear, the eye, touch, and kinesthetic 'sense', so uniquely important in learning. Thus

The Natural Order of Evaluation
1) Physico-chemical, electronic process,
    more important than:
2) The 'object', a nervous abstraction in the brain,
    more important than:
3) The verbal levels or descriptions,
    more important and reliable than:
4) Inferences of lower order,
    more important and reliable than:
5) Inferences of higher order,
    etc., etc.

It should be remembered that the simplest and most reliable descriptions are made in physico-mathematical languages and are closest to 'facts'; inferences, already being abstractions of higher orders, going away from 'facts', so that the higher order inferences we make, the less reliable they become. This applies to our *daily orientations* which are *not* scientific, but is not true about modern *exact sciences* where inferential data become more important than mere primitive, anthropomorphic, fictitious (as far as the outside world is concerned) 'sense data'.

We have established here a fundamental *Natural Order of Evaluation*, established by empirical inspection and observation of 'facts' of living and *SCIENCE*, which represents nothing but another form of HUMAN REACTIONS, and so becomes a form of living. Here 'time-binding' comes in, where accumulating 'racial experience' called "science" in *human* life, becomes in the main *more important* than *personal individual opinions*.

Here we have established a definite NATURAL, extra-neural, extra-personal, etc., order of evaluation, by *INSPECTION* of 'facts' of *actual living*, which INCLUDES *science*, as a 'fact' of human behavior and reactions. In the next lecture I will show you that our present orientations and semantic reactions are based on the *reverse order* of the *natural order of evaluation*. The worst of it is that our home as well as our educational methods in schools and universities, train us in this *pathological* reverse order of evaluation, under which *sanity* is made almost *impossible*.

Once we clarify these issues the future educational procedure is quite clear. For sanity's sake, for adjustment's sake, we must reverse the prevalent *reversed order* of NATURAL ORDER OF EVALUATION, and so we will prevent so-called 'mental' illnesses in youth, and eventually succeed in helping those already afflicted, dementia praecox, infantilism, included.

SEMINAR LECTURE TWELVE

Remember that our adjustment to life depends on predictability and that depends on similarity of structure. I have shown you that with elementalistic languages and non-elementalistic facts, we cannot get this predictability. Now we will investigate further the natural order of evaluation. We all have some special way of evaluating things and people, for example, this school, your friends, yourselves, or me. This is a personal evaluation. The question is whether it has any validity. We don't know, let's see. Without investigation, we cannot say whether your evaluation is appropriate. Otherwise, we have to investigate whether there are some factors of evaluation which are more valid than others. When we say *natural order of evaluation* that is something to be verified. Otherwise, we are getting a better hold on the factors of evaluation. If we can get that we have accomplished something. I want you to realize that we have come to a level of natural order of evaluation that can be verified, and then we have something solid to go by.

I will show you tonight that our daily standard of evaluation is the *reversal* of the *natural order of evaluation*. And the old psychotherapy, the 'curing' of the insane, goes that way because they deal with the reversed order too, and all we have to do is to restore the natural order. But this takes months and sometimes years to do. I tried to explain to you last lecture the problem of the natural order of evaluation. The physico-chemical make-up of an artificial apple would fit all so-called 'sense' perceptions and definitions, but that apple would not suit us. And yet, all so-called 'sense' perceptions would be covered. We would say it is an 'apple', but it is not. So the question which arises for us, as living beings, is to know that the physico-chemical processes, which we do not see, are more important than the objects we do see. Otherwise, the asymmetrical relation is more important. Never forget that asymmetrical relations are irreversible, for if you reverse them you are in trouble to begin with. Whenever you say that A is more than B, B is never more than A. You cannot reverse them. If you do reverse them, you are in a mess. Please remember some of the most important relations in the world are asymmetrical and we get in trouble if we reverse them. If we reverse the natural order of evaluation, we are not happy, adjusted, 'intelligent', etc.

I will go slow and please cooperate with me. This has to be taken slowly, it is so important. You as a class, have you ever thought that the physico-chemical process is more important than the object? Did it ever occur to you that this is of such importance? That the object does not matter but the physico-chemical process does matter? How do we evaluate, the rest of us? Did you ever hear of the importance of the physico-chemical process? What would you know about the object? Was *not* the *object* always *the most important thing to you*? Is that correct? No! Don't you see the *reversed order*? In *your evaluation* the object is *the most impor-*

Lecture Twelve

tant because you do not know better. Is that not so through life? How about your sweetheart, an object or a process? Do they differ from day to day? If you would realize the process character of a sweetheart would you be so often disappointed? I wonder if you see it? In the old way the object was the most important. Was that correct? Does that not reverse the natural order of evaluation? Is that sound?

I wish you would get this, that when you talk, say about your toothache, your toothache as you evaluate it, is unspeakable. Whatever you will *say*, will not be or cover the toothache. You must realize that when it comes to the 'feeling', what you directly 'feel' is not what you say. This is a very difficult thing to get. Say you like me or dislike me. Say I said something that makes you rebel, and you have a sore feeling about it. This happens in life. That direct feeling is not the same as what you say. We identify all the time. We identify direct feeling with the verbalism. In our direct feelings we identify the objective level with what we say and that is where the real trouble comes in. Now, talking about natural order of evaluation, let us talk about your toothache. I don't want to make you unhappy but I wish each of you had a toothache so you would know what I am talking about. That toothache, that you talk about, is not what you feel directly. When we express verbally the direct feelings, we often identify the toothache with the words. You make verbal statements and fancy they are your feelings. This is a very difficult thing to explain. We do not, or seldom, identify the *word* 'table' with that (pointing to a table). It begins with it, but this toothache is not so objective and when you talk about your toothache you identify the words with it; and words are *not* it. The '*objective*' feeling is a 'toothache', but behind that is a physico-chemical process. That is what is behind it as a 'causative' factor of the objective feeling of a toothache. I want to get that across to you, that your actual toothache has an *objective character*, but behind that there is the physico-chemical process going on. Remember we are talking about 'facts'. I hope you are getting the problem. When I say something you immediately break into verbalization, and get into trouble. You shout around and then you feel 'better', quotation marks. But, you just verbalize the feeling. We cannot make it the real *feeling*. So you see when we come to the field of direct personal feelings, we go by words, and disregard the actual issues. We apply more value to verbalization of the feelings than to the feelings themselves. The direct response or the *feeling* is more important than what you can say about it. You shivered when I slapped the girl's face in the slapping experiment because you were full of verbalistic doctrines to the opposite. Where you would shiver, someone else with another set of doctrines would not, and doctrines are verbal. Now, in daily life outside of tables, chairs, apples, etc., we always identify our verbalizations with our direct feelings. And, that is where the horror of the thing comes in because automatically then we do not evaluate direct feelings, but the verbalizing of them which *are not* the feelings.

Otherwise, when it comes to the natural order of evaluation, the feeling is *more important* than the verbal expression about it. We identify what we *say* with what we *feel*. And, in doing this, we do not have any delayed reactions. We ascribe more importance to the verbal level than to the objective level, and what matters in life is the objective level. That is the reverse order. Now give a description of anything, for example this girl here, she has a red dress. If I were color blind, that dress might be green. That is the subjective part of description. Every one of you sees things differently. This is subjectiveness! These are abstractions made up in your head. Now, when I have some descriptions, and then I begin to draw some inferences, the description of a so-called 'fact' is more reliable than the inference. We are dealing with evaluation either way, but the description is more important, more reliable, than the inference. Now if you have several orders of inferences, a lower order inference will be more reliable than a higher order inference. This is how the natural order of evaluation spreads. One level is more important than another. I was speaking about verbal doctrines of any sort. They are all different and inferences of high order. We do not react to descriptions, but rather to inferences as a basis for direct actions. Otherwise, in private life inferences are more important to us than descriptions. The whole thing is the reversal of the natural order, entirely the reverse.

In science we start with descriptions in the simplest terms. We do not do that as a life orientation. We start in the nursery being pumped full of misinformations. Our orientations go by higher order inferences that are entirely unreliable, because they follow from non-existent descriptions, fictitious descriptions, etc. You can imagine how healthy those inferences will be. The tragedy of our lives is where we live by the reversal of the natural order of evaluation. We must also realize the process character of 'matter' and the colloidal character of life. We do not know that, and have no business being in a college. That is modern nursery stuff, and you should know that.

Now I want to forewarn you. We have plenty of knowledge which we *never apply*. I will tell you something more. I have had students, university graduates, who knew as much physics and physiology as I did, but they never applied what they knew, and when I forced them to apply what they knew all along, they blew up. They could not stand it. They could not stand the application of what they knew all along. We are not so short of knowledge after all. We know a lot, but we seldom apply what we know. This goes all through life. I want you to be fully convinced and aware of the *natural order of evaluation*. You have to accept it or deny it. There is no choice but that. But, now don't just say "blah". Accept it or deny it.

Here then I say is the natural order of evaluation. Here I say the physico-chemical process is more important than the object. Then the object is more important than the description or definition; the description is more important than the inference; and finally, inferences of higher order are less important, less reliable, than inferences of lower orders. We live mostly by this reverse order. Do not think about yourselves as a white-collar class. Think about the billion and a half of humanity you never see or think about. They need this too. They know nothing about the physico-chemical processes, the colloidal processes, but only know about the object. The most important thing *to them* is the object. But, that is on the level of apes. You cannot convey GS to a gorilla. You

Lecture Twelve 175

see yourselves, the working difficulties you are having in getting that. And, yet you are high-grade white people. You can imagine how impossible it would be to convey all that to a gorilla. It would be impossible. Our nervous system has produced science and it will accept science. Our brain receives it, but the gorilla is unfit to receive science. The white man's brain is actually different, in colloidal structure and function from other brains. I have seen diagrams showing vascularity, that is blood vessels of the brain. If they took a high ape, for example a gorilla, and in a given portion of the brain, say, that fellow had five blood vessels, a primitive man in the same spot of the brain would have many times more blood vessels. Otherwise, different nutrition, food, energy. If you take a white idiot, he will have more blood vessels than the primitive man in that same spot. And then you take an adult white man, so-called 'normal', and the whole space, the same space, is literally filled with blood vessels. You can see how the amount of food the nervous system is getting, how the energy content of the productivity varies from one type to another. This is why you can understand when we speak about 'man' what idiotic fiction it is, when the nervous systems are so different.

Having covered the natural order of evaluation, let us pass now to a sort of generalized form of applying what we have had in the past lectures. We have stressed indefinitely standard stuff, there is nothing new about it; all I have said is old knowledge. First, that the organism works as-a-whole. We can never separate the organism, even as-a-whole, from the environment, from some sort of environment. Therefore, the formulation 'organism-as-a-whole' is not sufficient, because it does not include environment. This is why in GS we insist on the *non-elementalistic* treatment which is broader than the *organism-as-a-whole* business. We make efforts to formulate issues which include the environment. To those of you who are interested in a scholarly advance I again suggest that you read *Topological Psychology*, by Kurt Lewin. The topological methods, although they are respectable mathematical methods, had no application until this work. Topology is based on the relations between parts and wholes. You can read that book without any mathematical training. There is no orthodox mathematical technique there, but you will learn a general method of inclusion of parts in the whole which applies to everything human and yet it has a good mathematical method behind it. Talk about broadness, it is the broadest application yet of mathematics and extensional methods to human life. This book breaks the ice. So the nervous system not only works as-a-whole, but the external and *internal* environment must be included. And today we have learned something more which is fundamental but hidden behind antiquated verbiage. Professor Parker of Harvard has shown, experimentally, that the nerve endings produce what he calls some sort of hormones. You know what hormones are, secretions from glands. That verbiage complicates somewhat the nervous issues. We cannot talk in the terms of hormones, or gland secretions at the ends of nerves. Apply correct English to the situation. There is no gland at the end of a nerve. We have no right to talk about the hormones at the end of a nerve, but how about the colloids? Nerves conduct electrical currents. At the end of the nerve then there would be some charge or rather some definite polarity; and if you have polarity, and a current passes down the nerve, you would have a new colloidal configuration. It would act as a bit of a 'chemical' process. But you cannot isolate it, for it stops as soon as you block the current, but at the moment it can act as a chemical, perhaps *like* a hormone. There are subtle differences, but you can see to what extent they become complicated and to what degree we must consider them before we can take care of the problems as they loom up.

So, coming to the nervous system we must take the organism-as-a-whole. As-a-whole in every sense, in every important detail we know. That is why you cannot disregard the environment as it is ordinarily understood. Air, water, etc., are all part of the environment. You cannot get away from a neuro-linguistic and neuro-semantic environment either, something that has been entirely disregarded. Can you imagine yourself for a second without a neuro-semantic environment? We cannot be free from some sort of evaluation. Our whole life is full of some sort of evaluation. We have some standards of evaluation in spite of the fact that we might not know it consciously, for we act on them.

From embryology (remember all I say now is elementalistic) we know that the eye is not a 'sense' organ. In the embryo we start with a little lump which is in our nervous system; then we see that getting elongated. From the lump it elongates and turns out to be the eye. The eye is not a so-called 'organ' but it happens to be a direct part of the brain. There is no such thing as what we call the 'optic nerve'. There is only an *optic tract* which directly connects the outside part of the brain, which is the eye, with the rest of the brain. This does not apply to your other 'sense' organs though. This is one of the reasons why in our white civilization all our sciences have been ultimately brought under the control of the eye. All our instruments of any description are arranged for eye control. Even if we deal with hearing we try to bring the instruments under the control of the eye. The *outside* part of the *actual* brain is our eye. That is why the best learning is through the eye, and that is why so-called 'visualization' is the main factor in adjustment; why the highest so-called forms of human 'thinking' are visual 'thinking', just because through visualization we are directly dealing with the brain. It turns out for instance that animals are much more 'ear-minded' than 'eye-minded'. And we, the higher order of intelligence, so often are 'visual-minded'. An *extensional* fellow would be 'eye-minded'. An *intensional* fellow would be 'ear-minded'. By extension we formulate everything to the eye in terms of order, in terms of enclosures of parts in a whole. That is, we use topological methods. Through indexes and dates we cover up processes in terms of separation, and so we are capable of passing from dynamic to static and static to dynamic. Do not forget that the linguistic centers are definitely cortical. The cortex with its linguistic intensional definitions has static definitions; and the thalamus is dynamic. In the meantime all I say is wrong because in speech I have to separate them, but they do not act separately. The moment you realize that what I say is wrong, we can have some sort of understanding. Do you get that? If you would take what I say literally, I would misguide you. *The organism does not work in separate parts.* In teaching youngsters, we have to stress that the old verbiage will not cover the facts, and mostly falsifies them. This is where the extensional devices come in. For our purposes here, we choose to talk in terms of the separation of the cortex from the thalamus, but I must forewarn you that that is wrong. And yet from such an orientation useful knowledge appears. The linguistic centers are in the cortex and by necessity of the old intension, they are static. We make a definition, which we use for the time being until we change it, so it is static. Now life, as well as a piece of iron, is a process. Although iron is a slower process than life, it is a process just the same. Some processes are much faster than others. The difference between all the processes in the world is only in their duration. Everything under the sun, as we know it today, is a process and therefore dynamic. Language is static, but we have means today to reconcile the dynamic world with the static language. By extension we have the means to reconcile them.

Now, if the intensional language is static but the world dynamic, there is no similarity in structure in the old way. But now we have means to reconcile them by using the extensional devices and four-dimensional methods. For, the moment you index and date a passing event you have a four-dimensional cross section that is static. This is four-dimensional, remember. A process can be made static in four dimensions. If you have a 'chair' as a definition, that is static, but when you exhibit by extension, you exhibit things, $chair_1$, $chair_2$, $chair_3$, etc.; you have any number of chairs. You have made 'chair' dynamic — changing. We can then readjust the structure of the static language to the dynamic world. These issues are important, and the ignorance of them is tragic. Let me ask you a question. I challenge anybody here, staff included, to give me the name of one scientist, of world fame or not, who is 'scientific[1937]'. This is serious. There is *no one*. Even an Einstein will not fit. He has done his great work, but he knows nothing about neurology, psychiatry, GS, etc. He cannot deal with neurology in a scientific way. Then we cannot say he is 'scientific[1937]'. You students here are more scientific[1937] than Einstein himself because you are getting the fundamental rudiments of methods and 'facts' from all branches of science, not merely one.

I am glad you got this static-dynamic business as well as you did. Remember that the thalamus, which is the dynamic center in us, is full of dynamic reactions. Let me give you an example of a moving picture film. In a moving picture we have a living scene, when it is running in three plus one dimensions. Now, we stop the motion (this is the four-dimensional static cross section) and you will have static pictures. The loves, or hates, that before were moving are now seen in static cross sections. You blend them together by motion and you have a living affair, but you stop the film and you have only static cross sections, measurable static jerks.

Measurements in this world are very important just because they are extensional, that is all. And, in measurement, miracles happen, miracles which you could not foresee. For instance, imagine you are flat, two-dimensional people. If you fancy you are flat beings, you would say that the third dimension is 'beyond' you. Now I will show you what happens. You are on the surface of the earth (E): incidentally, the earth being curved, is three dimensional, but you do not

$\pi = 3.1415...$ etc.

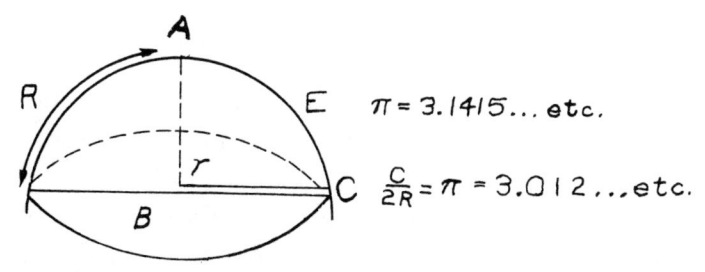

$\frac{C}{2R} = \pi = 3.012...$ etc.

understand three dimensions if you are flat, and you legitimately say that the third dimension is 'beyond' you. You begin to measure and now see what happens. You make a circle (C) with radius (R) on the curved earth, and actually measure its circumference on the *curved* earth. Then you measure the actual radius (R). You know something about the geometric symbol "pi" (π) do you not? By *actual measurement* of this circle (C) you have made and the actual radius (R) we calculate π: it would be *less* than 3.1415, etc., which value π =3.1415... applies to a *flat surface*. But here you do not know whether you deal with a flat surface or not because you are two-dimensional yourself. You are going ahead by actually measuring (C) you have drawn on the earth's surface with radius (R), which is curved, not (r), and measuring (R). If your measurement of (R) is larger than the (r) of a flat circle (B), then your new π would be less than the π =3.1415... in two dimensions. Your two dimensional, flat being, through *actual measurement* then would find out there would be a third dimension, because your old 'pi' will be greater than the new 'pi' by actual measurement of (C) and (R).

Remember this is a sort of 'miracle'. Through *measurement* alone we have reached the notion of a *new dimension*. Otherwise, there is something in measurement that has an extraordinary revealing power. It goes further than this but it is obvious that your two-dimensional beings have gotten a glimpse of a third dimension by measurement even though it is 'beyond' you because you are two-dimensional. Now the secret of it is extensional treatment. That is the secret of all measurement, and here we come to the secret of numbers, the definition of numbers.

The old definition of number was that they were a "class of classes". If you have a series of couples, that is not a 'number'; if you say two apples that is not a 'number' either; but when you abstract from all couples, and you abstract from it the *number two* they call that a "class of classes", a class of all couples. Now if you explore the world with the old "number", otherwise a "class of classes", you may just as well explore the world with the 'holy ghost'; for you will get answers in terms of a 'class of classes' or the 'holy ghost' and you know nothing about the world when you get back to some sense. You do not learn much by using such definitions. But, now imagine that you treat a number as a *relation*, that is a new semantic definition of number, and you explore the world with *relations* you will be getting answers in *terms of relations*, not 'holy ghosts'. You will have answers in terms of relations and they become *factors of structure*. And the only thing we can know is structure, formulated in terms of relations. You can begin to see the importance of certain terminology. Its importance for the building of a science and exploring this world, and ourselves.

We were talking about the eye and the nervous system before, and we said that the eye is a part of the brain. You can realize now that a *relation* of any sort can be made *visual* if we know how. Every kind of *relation* can be formulated to your *eye* as a visual issue. Otherwise, by reformulating old notions into a structural language as bundles of relations, static or dynamic, we are getting formulations which can be made visual. We have means to directly influence the cortex and the brain, because we are dealing with the eye which is itself a part of the brain. Other benefits are that some unteachable things in this old way now become teachable. I will explain that on the basis of this diagram called the Structural Differential. There is a good diagram of this in my book, *Science and Sanity*, and it must be studied. This Structural Differential here represents the structural differences and natural order of evaluation. Many of my friends fancy that I am cranky about this Structural Differential, but some of my best students understand that for getting full benefit out of extensionalization it is impossible without actual playing with diagrams and charts like this. This is a fundamental point of extensionalization, because it affects the thalamus as well as the cortex.

Everything goes through the thalamus, and so the eye. That is the importance of working with charts and diagrams and models. The parabola at the top of this model represents a process, the holes represent a part of the infinite number of characteristics of that process. In an ever-changing process an event has an infinite number of characteristics. This is a *static representation* of a *dynamic process*. This is a static cross section of an endless process. The event, in science, after Einstein-Minkowski is a cross section of a four-dimensional

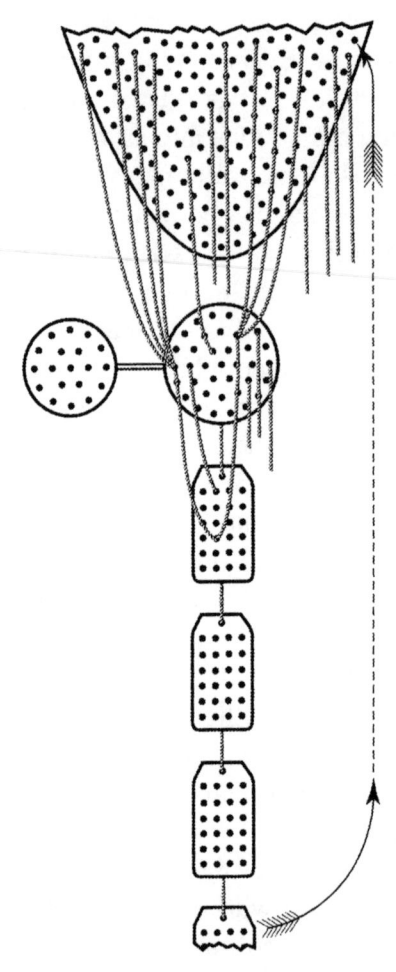

process which is *static at an instant*. In the meantime there is the physico-chemical process going on just the same. As this is a static representation we have to have the event here, and to make it visual and static we have to ascribe to it an infinite number of characteristics. These are the holes in the model. Now, you remember that our nervous system abstracts a disk out of rotating blades. Well, here is the object, abstracted from the event. The object has a finite number of characteristics. We do not abstract all the characteristics of the event. Here in the diagram we see some holes without strings, also some strings *not* connected with the object, 'characteristics left out' of our abstractions. Our nervous system builds up the object but we never abstracted all the characteristics of the 'object'. We always have characteristics left out. Then we label the object like we label a trunk, just a mere label which is only a name or a definition. When we have reached this level of labeling or speaking, we can *speak about speaking*, in other words we abstract in higher orders, etc. That is the next level on this diagram, below the object. Then we see the whole nature of the natural order of evaluation, *conveyed by the eye*. (Pointing to the Differential.) This is more important than that, and this is more important than that, etc. The top of the model, the event, is more important than the object, the object more important than the description, description more important than inferences of lower and higher orders, etc. This is the value of the Differential. We *visualize* the *natural order of evaluation*. You may not realize it but this order of importance is common knowledge, but in the meantime it is very seldom applied, that the so-called kinesthetic movements have such a great influence on our brains. This is why I definitely advise you to use your hands at present; follow this advice because I want you to get results. You have definite orders of abstractions, different levels of abstractions, scientific verbal inferences on different levels. When you deal with objects, a chair, me, or yourself, you must use your hands ordering your individuals. Don't you feel how you shake yourself into order, $Smith_1$, $Smith_2$, etc., and that shaking of and ordering by the hand affects the thalamus, and when you talk about $Smith_1$, $Smith_2$, etc., move your hands. It will help you establish the order of your evaluation. That little wiggle really does the trick. It will help you.

First, I showed you the orderings of the absolute individuals; now here comes the ordering of orders of abstractions. You have a two fold, four-dimensional stratification and when you shake your self in that ordered series of abstractions, you are inwardly ready to map a successful adjustment. You have the secret of clarity, all of which is not verbal. It becomes organismal and kinesthetic. That is when you become stratified in four dimensions. You have added acuteness to your brain. You have engaged yourself organically into thinking, more than just using your 'brain'. Then you begin to orientate yourself as-a-whole, which is non-elementalistic. You reach your best self because you approach yourself through the eye, the ear, the kinesthetic 'sense', etc., all by training yourself in extension with the differential.

This is no fad. It is the only method at present of getting at these things, and influencing the thalamus. Here we are conveying to you the secret of 'wisdom', etc. We have brought knowledge to your brain, not only through the ear, but the eye, touch, and the whole of kinesthetic 'senses'.

SEMINAR LECTURE THIRTEEN

I am very pleased with the results of the lectures and the private conferences I have been having. This means that extensionalization works; some things are beginning to click. Some results are very good. Remember I have stressed all this time the similarity of structure. My aim in stressing this similarity of structure is predictability. Now those who have gone through the seminar and have had private conferences realize the great importance of predictability. Therefore, if we can get some factors of predictability, we will be better off. And predictability depends on similarity of structure, and this depends on multi-dimensional order. You do not need to understand multi-dimensionality perfectly just yet. A little bit will be helpful. We are coming to the end of the Seminar, so I want to convey to you not only theoretical issues but also their application. For instance, the extensional mechanisms, and how to apply them. By the way, do not treat me as a lecturer talking to students. I am having a colloidal nervous jazz trying to reproduce similar colloidal jazzes in your nervous systems. All action is by contact. There is a long chapter about this in my book. Read it. In our new world there is no 'empty space' either. We are living in a world of *fullness*. It makes for an entirely different orientation. We are not living in an empty world. Thus we cannot even talk about political 'isolation'. We have in our papers stock market reports from the markets in London, Paris, New York, etc., and still we talk about 'isolation'. It is time to stop that. We really are not isolated. This applies everywhere. A discovery is made somewhere, a discovery of an important character, and we are all affected by it. Don't you see how 'isolation' has no place in the human world? This 'isolation' follows from the notion of 'emptiness of space'. We can exist no longer and preserve sanity under such conditions. Otherwise, what we must do now is to get hold of scientific facts, coordinate them, and extract methods from them and then use those methods for making new orientations.

Since this is next to the last lecture, if you do not understand, ask me to repeat. You see to begin with if I had been just a mere verbalist, a speaker to hearers, I would not have done what I did. I would not have been interested in you. I would have said my say, and you heard it, and that is that. That is the verbalistic attitude, but by extension, I am interested in *you*, in *your colloidal jazzes*. I deal by *contact* with my *colloidal jazzes* and yours. I would not be satisfied if nothing happened. Neurologically and colloidally, it is not all over when you do not get something from the speaker. This is very important for the educational staff here to realize. We have permanent difficulties between teachers and students; namely, a teacher delivered his lecture the best he could. He "did his job". Now the question is of the reaction of the student to what he heard. It is individual to begin with and it is not enough for the teacher to say and the pupil to hear. That does not work, as you know. You

Lecture Thirteen

have received through your training special colloidal jazzes in your nervous system, and if you cannot convey that colloidal jazz to the student, you have not accomplished anything. Then you complain about the difficulties of education because you orient yourself intensionally. Extensionally you are not a teacher to a student, you are a neurological colloidal jazz, transforming the neurological colloidal jazzes of your students. If you do not accomplish that, you have accomplished nothing as an educator. This is one of the great difficulties of education and here mass-education fails because we deal with large classes. And, then we speak about students as morons, feebleminded, etc. That is wrong, for our *attitude* is wrong; the fact is that you as well as students represent colloidal jazzes, and education works only as far as we educators can transpose our colloidal jazzes to students' colloidal jazzes. You have seen the colloidal attitude of an extensional teacher who will not go ahead until something is gotten by the class. This is generally what I do. This extensional method should be the foundation of all education, for then teachers must have the non-elementalistic extensional attitude. Don't you see the difference between extension and intension? In that connection I want to show you a rather scandalous difference between an extensional attitude and an intensional one.

Go back to that diagram of happiness. In it your expectation should be minimum of 'maximum probability'. I will now prove to you *verbally* that I produced a most 'destructive, criminal theory of happiness' which will be destructive to 'civilization', etc. First let us take it from an intensional angle. You are familiar with the expression, "masturbation of the salivary glands". Well, I will do some of that now and I want your opinion. I want your opinion as discriminating between two different opinions. You will not be able to prick a hole in the intensional argument. I will 'prove' that the theory is destructive and then we will make another analysis which is *extensional* which *reverses* the whole business.

Well, we start with *minimum expectation*, that is the *new* orientation. "Expect nothing". We might say that if we expect nothing, we will want nothing, we will accomplish nothing, etc. That is an *intensional* argument, but is that *verbal* argument correct? You cannot prick a hole in that argument just the same. It is destructive, just killing. You will want nothing, you will strive for nothing, you will not look for anything. Notice how far we can go on with that verbally. That is the intensional 'criminality' of the happiness theory. Verbally, by *intension*, you cannot find a loophole in such a verbal argument.

I am giving you now some short summaries of the sort of difficulties you will find yourself exposed to. I am suggesting to you arguments by presenting this *intensional* argument, a verbal argument, which you cannot prick verbally. By *intension*, verbally you can condemn our theory of happiness.

Now, let us look at extensional '*facts*', never mind verbal masturbation. Analysis by 'facts' whatever kind of 'facts' we have, represents an extensional analysis. Now let us analyze 'facts'. As a matter of fact (indicating a student), here is a fellow who may sometimes starve me, but he usually brings me my meals. We may smile but we are dealing with 'facts'. I tell you a joke, for instance, and you break into laughter about it, because somehow you have made an *extensional* analysis about it. You have reconstructed the facts about it. In the joke, the words say nothing, but the contrast — territory: the facts; map: language — made you laugh. You have reconstructed the facts, and the laughter comes from an *extensional* reconstruction of the facts *behind* the words. The moment we reconstruct facts behind the word sounds, life orientations begin. This is an example of a difference in orientation by which unfortunately we will make an extensional orientation about a joke, but we will not do this when serious life problems are concerned. One of the reasons is that we know so little about life in general. The joke example is easy to reconstruct. But, life is not so simple to readjust, or to reconstruct.

So then I have shown you the *destructive* character of the extensional theory of happiness as made up by *intensional analysis*. Now let us see facts. Here is a living being (exhibiting an actual student), remember a living being, pulsating with life, having a lot of *impacts* with facts of environment. We cannot not do that and not be a fiction. None of us can be eliminated from the environment and still exist. Disregard it and you have a fiction. A living being cannot be eliminated from the environment. None of us can get away from a semantic and a linguistic environment either. Well then, here is the living being. He has impacts with the environment. Eating, drinking, etc., he cannot get away from these, and that means you, remember. I contemplate *this individual*; you make your analysis on *individuals*, $Smith_1$, $Smith_2$, etc. I keep this young fellow up here before the class because I have to have an individual something here to talk about. An individual. By *intension*, I talk generalizations, false to facts perhaps, as by *intension* we force facts into generalizations. But by *extension*, we contemplate individuals and then make our own hypothetical orientations and generalizations. Now I am showing you the *extensional* theory of happiness. *Intensionally* I have proved to you the 'criminality' of it, how it is destructive to civilization, etc. We have minimum expectation, but if we expect nothing we will get nothing, etc. Now let's see. I teach this actual boy to expect the *maximum*, but if his expectation is maximum, he expects good water here, and he gets this actual one, he will be disappointed. Of course, if he expects 'good water', and he gets this iron-water that I have in this glass; he would be disappointed. But, if he expects some sort of mud from this glass and gets the *actual* iron-water, he will be *more than satisfied*. Remember he is a living fact and remains a fact. You know that the water here is not tasty and so do I. But if he *expects crystal clear water*, etc., and gets this (indicating), he will not be satisfied with that (indicating). But if he is *prepared* for something still worse, he will be glad to have this water. This is not joking.

How about facts? I am *satisfied* since my expectation is still worse than this actual water. If my expectation inwardly, semantically, was still worse than the extensional water, I am not made unhappy. Now remember that in the GS seminars we are brutally frank, and when we have foolish things going on with ourselves, we admit them. Now I was talking about physical expectation about that water. I expected worse than the actual water and this time (drinking), it did not taste so badly. I am showing you, in a living being, the semantic tricks. It is a sort of confession. But believe me, if I had expected a crystal water out of this glass, I would be very disappointed.

Remember the *intensional* argument where "minimum expectation ruins happiness". From birth up, we can never escape some teachings. We can never escape the implication of the *structure* of language. Imagine I train you, and it means from the cradle up, I am supposedly your "pa" or "ma". Just suppose that. Now I am training you in an *elementalistic* language. The structure of the language that says 'body' and 'mind' *can be separated* which is not correct from a life point of view. So, in teaching you an elementalistic language, I teach you some consequences that are unnoticed, yet false to fact. I teach you a vicious intensional orientation by verbal definitions, that things are *not* individual but generalities. You cannot avoid consequences with that sort of intensional teaching. This is where the *structure of language* comes in. Because the *structure of language involves* and *implies structure.* It is impossible to teach one thing without teaching something else. You will understand that later. Let us suppose that this boy is, or that you are, illiterate and you remain illiterate. Then I teach you some religion that involves automatically some physics, some biology, etc.; I am teaching you something structurally definite when I teach you language alone of certain structure. What I am trying to stress is that you cannot help but learn something when they teach you a language of certain structure, *just a language.* When I teach you language, I am *teaching you something besides language.* When I am *not* telling you that there are four or five meanings to "apples" behind the word "apple", I am training you in *confusion*, in *identifications*, although I was only supposed to be giving you a language lesson. To be trained in the nursery in a language of a false-to-fact structure is to get *false orientations through necessary implications*. This is unavoidable. This is why I am speaking about a *semantic environment*, because if you know it or not, if you teach only ordinary language, by the structure of language, you train the child in false-to-fact world orientations. You are training him in *false knowledge*; you are *preparing him for maladjustment*. Now let us go back to that theory of happiness.

I do this deliberately so you could see actually the performance of an *extensional* analysis. In the *intensional* analysis the theory is 'defective and destructive'. Now let us see the evaluation by *extension*. Here again is the same living being. He is just born. He is not free from environment. I am his "pa", say, training him in *some language*. This is *not* so-called 'official education', we are both of a low order of slum people. I have, as a matter of fact, to train him in *some* language. In the old way I would train him in the *vernacular*, which is *elementalistic* and *intensional*. I would train him in *false knowledge*, preparing him for maladjustment and whatnot, just because I am training him automatically in false knowledge. For when I train him in language of elementalistic and intensional structure, I am training him in false knowledge. Remember there is no 'science' or 'education' in this training. He is illiterate and so am I. We cannot deal intelligently with anything by intension. This automatic working cannot be avoided on the lowest level when we train in a language of elementalistic and intensional structure. That is not a correct representation of facts without indexes, dates, etc. Such 'education' without some form of 'science' can wreck life. I am training him now in a theory of happiness of maximum expectation. This fellow standing here is wiggling his fountain pen. (Keep on doing what you were doing, playing with that pen.) That is really nothing much to it, but it is not the best thing to do. Here I pick on that because it is so innocent, but I am having maximum expectations and I am heartbroken, and I say: "Look at what he is doing. Oh! Dear me!" I had *maximum expectations.* I will knock him down and beat him. I will be one of those people, one of those parents who expect too much. I will nag him. Dementia praecox or paranoia will be the result, because he knows by himself that I am a fool to nag him, but he will not tell me so. I know this example matters so little but I have a maximum expectation, and he is nagged for that. I build up maladjustment in him. Remember I now exhibit life here, no definitions. He did something that we all do, but with my maximum expectation it made me unhappy and I nagged him, driving him ill.

Now you have seen here a picture of my maximum expectation. I picked on something innocent, and made a mess out of his life and mine. I may add that unexpectedly in a great many neurotic parents, maximum expectation has made the child neurotic. Most nagging comes from too many expectations. We would nag everyone if we expected too much. Now, let's go back to the *minimum expectation.* Here is the same living being; I am the same and our relations are between two living beings. I ask him up before the class.

Understand he has some weaknesses, so do I. I have *minimum* expectation. Now I train him in minimum expectation and to evaluate his environment with maximum *probability* and so some *predictability* of a scientific character. He will bump against extensional facts in life, and as a living being, he will have inside reactions to those facts. He will find facts 'better' than his expectations; his reactions will be hopeful, not hopeless; he will feel like going up in life; he will not be frightened by life, etc. That is the living being, and we are reversing the theory of maximum expectation. By extension we are always 'happy' because we go to the facts. Remember that if I would have a sick liver I would find everything 'bad', only because my liver was sick. This is how that works. When you have maximum expectation everything is 'bad'. Now, see what I have done. I have explored the world. I treated my parents extensionally. My "mother" was only "the woman who had borne me", nothing more, and so, I had no family troubles. I would help her if she was in trouble, but, I would not have inside 'feelings', 'emotions', 'upsets', over her. Extensionally remember. That is the trouble with many of you. You are intensional with your "pa" and "ma". You are still infantile. When you are involved personally by intension, you make yourself and others miserable. But when you are free, extensional, you do not make yourself miserable. By freeing yourself extensionally you will be your own age. Few of you in this room are your own age. You must realize how hates can be manufactured, just by that difference in attitude. Your affects, feelings, and energies are limited, so you will not have energy left for positive feelings if you only hate. We call the results of this overflowing of hate dementia praecox. If hate does not overrun you completely, but you hate, you may be a good hater. If you are too tied up it is likely you will be infantile. You are 'everything' to "pa" and "ma". This is how intensional attitudes manufacture tragedies in life. These tragedies are not really necessary. I am showing you the mechanisms by which happiness and maladjustment are manufactured. If we are 'unhappy', we are unable to give 'happiness' to the other fellow. In bad cases of family troubles I advise the students not to use the terms "father" and "mother" but call them Mr. Smith and Mrs. Smith. Very often the difficulties disappear. We are biological units, $Smith_1$, $Smith_2$, $Smith_3$, etc., and then there is no place for generalized resentment, hatred, etc., and we will be more kind, etc.

Some wise person, I do not remember who, once said: "A great many family troubles would be avoided if we could be as polite and as civilized with the members of the family as with strangers." We are not because we have too many expectations, etc. We say: "This boy is my flesh, my blood. Therefore, something must happen." When it does not happen we are broken-hearted. Many troubles are made this way. I wanted to convey to you the extensional analysis. I was taking $Smith_1$, $Smith_2$, $Smith_3$, etc., and their relationships as *living beings*, their reactions as *living beings*, *not* as definitions and generalizations.

By definitions and intension such an analysis would not be possible. Extensional analysis of 'facts' and reactions makes it possible. And, what I was explaining is very orthodox. That analysis is social, it is sound, and it should appeal. It is extensional. We do not fool ourselves by verbalism. We go by 'facts' concerning ourselves as individuals who react and act. The whole thing takes a different character. I tried to show you the difference between an intensional and an extensional analysis. We must reverse the old intensional stuff. Here individuals, not just definitions of "man", or "child" were taken into consideration. A living being acts and reacts as an individual not as an intensional definition. I wanted to show you how our old type of analysis has changed by this change in method.

We were speaking about the "similarity of structure". I told you that the organism acts as-a-whole, and that the nervous system acts and reacts as-a-whole, that the nervous division of the cortex and the thalamus is *functionally fictitious*, and that we cannot really separate them but only speak of them as if we could. Direct living and direct contact with the outside world is mostly thalamic, do you remember that? Now, the problem is that the thalamus, being in direct contact with the impact of the environment, is getting over-stimulated. That is why we are getting nervous and neurotic, because we do not have a properly trained cortex that will regulate the thalamus. It is over-stimulated from childhood up. The cortex control is small when the child is young, an over-stimulation occurs, and the thalamus is affected permanently and infantile organismal effects may become permanent. Now, if the nervous system and the organism-as-a-whole work as-a-whole, the best method of teaching would be not by *one* nerve center, but by *all available* nerve centers. I want to show you today the translation of our fundamental three premises into methods available and applicable to other nerve centers. I will tell you quite an illustrative and, in a way, a dramatic story of the discovery or invention of that method. [About 1922] I was lecturing to a high-grade institution of higher learning in New York. Lecturing on the same program with me were two important scientists. I knew a great deal depended on my carrying my point and I was under great tension. I was considered then a 'dreamer' and an 'idealist', still 'unscientific' from the old delusional point of view. Now I knew that those men were intensional and metaphysical and dealt with definitions, not with facts. I was very tense and on top of that a friend played a very mean trick on me. So I was not only tense but was greatly disturbed actually, even visibly. I wanted to convey there what I am conveying to you. I wanted to convey that in two hours to a very critical group, but I did not have the technique I have now. I did not yet have the semantic methods of extensionalization, etc. And then, under that pressure, I sketched for the first time the Structural Differential, the visual thalamic statement of the premises and explained to them the difference between *human world* and an *animal world*. This is the world of the animal (showing on the Differential), see on the model here. It is not connected with the event, the physico-chemical process, because Fido does not 'know' and *cannot know* that he only abstracts in a few orders of abstractions. This is a dramatic reproduction of what I told them. So this was really the whole beginning of GS. Creative work is always produced that way. You 'get it' first, and then spend a lifetime verbalizing it. These three premises of extension, all of them are negative to begin with, which means in accordance with modern science where the negative issues, where something is *not so*, are much more important than the 'positive'. The *positive theories are hypothetical*. Negative results show a theory to be wrong and the negative become the positive results. Would you call this light here a positive result? Yes? I am sorry, we are mistaken, *negative electrons* run it. That negative-positive business is optional, of course, but what we believed in the old days to be positive, turns out to be negative and vice versa. How do you like that?

The human brain has been built by negative reactions of 'delayed reactions'. The animal has immediate positive response, or reflex-reactions, and it remains a dog, a cat, a cow, etc. The brain and the cortex have been built by delayed ('negative') reactions. This is where the reversal comes in. Look at the premises. They are negative. And today in all modern science we know that the only *positive* theories we have are *negative* and the positive theories are only hypothetical. This means not only passing from an 'objective' anthropomorphic orientation to a *process orientation*, it means a *complete revision*. Remember the moment we face a 'fact' and a *mechanism* then we can handle them. So in GS if I had not doubted the doubt, I could not have been successful in my work. Perhaps I would be a more pleasant fellow, but the reason for my success is that I had *second order doubt*: I *doubted my own doubt*.

Here we come to the *multiordinality* of mechanisms that are so workable. Now first let us go back to the mechanisms. The first is that the map *is not* the territory. I will now talk 'baby talk' to you. But I will speak about solid facts in spite of it being 'baby talk'. (Showing on the Differential.) This is not this, and this on the diagram is not this, etc. Is that conveyed to you by the eye? Do you not see it is the denial of the "is" of identity? We are establishing through the eye, the kinesthetic sense, etc., that fact, that this is not this. You have this in the book. Look it over, read it. Otherwise, through all available 'senses' we are translating here the first premise. Now the second premise is that the map covers *not all* of the territory. The holes and the loose strings which you can see with the eye here on the Differential represent those characteristics *left out*. That conveys to you the 'not all'. Visualize that diagram and play with it. Those holes and unconnected strings here represent the 'not all'. Conveyed through the eye, touch, and kinesthetic senses, this diagram conveys to *all available 'senses'* the principles of the three premises. And then comes the problem of self-reflexiveness

This is a large problem and is the key of fundamental difficulties in life as well as science. Not in all, in an unlimited way, but in *all we know about*. I will summarize again the problem of self-reflexiveness. It may sound to you a little bit too abstract. In application you will find it is very close to life and you will find the problem not only affecting every phase of our life, but at the bottom of most difficulties we have. This problem ruined the foundation of mathematics and they had to invent the theory of types to patch up the foundation of mathematics. We can have no hope for the solution of human affairs if we cannot get a decent foundation for mathematics. There can be no economics, no sociology, etc., of any validity, if we cannot even get a sound foundation for mathematics. This is treated more fully in *Science and Sanity*. Remember the simple barber story?

In fact, it was discovered by a mathematician, and is connected with the theory of mathematical types. This story shows the messes we can make out of the old verbiage. This is a serious problem. I will give you another. The story of a problem that is 2300 years old, called the Zeno Paradox, about a race between a tortoise and Achilles. We have had this before. The tortoise was given a handicap. So here was Achilles and here was the tortoise (gesturing), which you know is not true. But I will 'prove' it to you and you try to disprove it. I want to give you some more shocks about language. Before Achilles can pass the tortoise he will have to halve the distance, then halve that half, and so on and he will never be able to reach or overrun the tortoise. Is that not tragic? But now try to make a hole in that argument.

The problem of self-reflexiveness in the meantime is more important. And, it is more simple. The difficulty of the barber was really in the formulation of the problem. It is tricky. However, this problem with Achilles is not tricky. But the barber problem can be solved quite simply. In my book this is explained under the theory of types. The mathematicians have solved the problem of self-reflexiveness through the theory of types. This is a great advance but it is yet not complete. In the old way we had that problem of self-reflexiveness at the point that if the barber "shaved himself", he "did not shave himself". So we had to have something to solve that verbal issue. It is the theory of types by Bertrand Russell. See the preface to *Principia Mathematica*, by Whitehead and Russell. It should interest many of you. You must get this for if you do not realize the dangers and pitfalls of language you will never get the importance of the need for the revision of the structure of language. Here in GS without any hitch and without difficult theories but only with extensional devices, by *extension*, we can handle those problems.

You ask me by intension: "Do you want a cigarette?" I say "yes", by intension. My "yes" by intension would be a "yes" by definition. Now my "yes" by intension would mean, say, "agreement" in general. It has no life content.

By intension it was 'general agreement', whatever you meant by it. So you have one general "yes" and it has no life content. But ask me extensionally whether I want a smoke, by extension. That has life content. The extensional life content of my "yes" is this smoke. You can see it. That is what this "yes$_1$" means in life as an extensional fact. Now you ask me another question, "Do you want a drink?" I say the same combination of letters, "yes". But the *content* is different. Thus extensionally, we have different contents to the "yes" which is always spelled the same way, but their content is different. By extension then, we have *many* "yeses", Yes$_1$, Yes$_2$, etc. In addition, terms like "yes" are multiordinal. I will speak more of the multiordinality of terms later. You can see how the indexes, etc., are an automatic solution of multiordinality, and also the mathematical theory of types.

SEMINAR LECTURE FOURTEEN

I am a little bit late, for my electrical razor developed suddenly some non-aristotelian, non-euclidean, and non-newtonian difficulties.

In finishing the seminar I will stress the last, and in fact the first and last point of GS. GS has been the result of the study of modern science and mathematics. It is a methodological study based on observations that human adjustment, sanity — call it "morals" if you will — all are at the best steadily declining. It has been estimated that in two hundred years there will be no sane white man left, and that does not take into account the constant acceleration of the tendency. It has been found that the spread of infantilism is also alarming. It has been found that existing educational methods are not satisfactory; instead of training for adjustment, the opposite occurs. Present education does not help adjustment. They teach you facts and details which we often are not interested in, but they do not teach us scientific method and how to adjust ourselves to the conditions of this world. Books have been rather recently written that are very valuable on things that every *modern* man should know. But in the meantime, in our schools we are throwing out much of mathematics and physics. Instead of giving nurseries and elementary schools the physico-mathematical methods which are *necessary* and most useful, we are throwing them out even in higher schools.

If you would see the structure of wood skeletons that are used in building a subway, see them taking out some dirt somewhere to use elsewhere, etc., etc., you would wonder at the brain work it takes to figure out all those details. It takes a lot of brain work. But when everything is *finished*, and we have only a tube with two or four lines of rails in it, we can take a small child through the tube, and he will tell you 'all about' the tube. It has become so 'simple'. What was a most elaborate affair to build becomes very simple when finished. Take a skyscraper. The material, the metal parts are all calculated, brought in and set up. And it is a most elaborate affair, difficult, laborious, complex, etc., but when that skyscraper is *finished*, a small child can be taken up into it and he will be at home in it. He will understand the inside of the skyscraper, and "that is that". A finished structure is usually simple.

The parallel applies directly to science and to us. You are supposedly 'scientific'. The techniques of sciences are like the scaffoldings of subways, skyscrapers, etc. The scaffoldings are elaborate and difficult to calculate, but the finished results are always simple. That is what seems easy, that is what we must understand. The *results* of science are always simple. Remember what I told you about the dynamic theory of 'matter'. It took endless work and endless techniques to develop this, to discover that 'matter' is not 'solid' but a process, only a "disk made up of rotating blades". But, that picture is not difficult to understand the moment facts are discovered: *we are told it is so.* It is just as simple as a finished skyscraper or a subway. The building of it was not simple, the discovery of the facts of physics were laborious and not simple, but the results are always simple. You remember what I told you about colloids. The known data about colloids are tremendous, and often colloids behave bafflingly. But the foundation of colloids as has been explained to you is quite simple. If you would know the amount of scientific work behind what little I have told you, you would be amazed. Really, even I am amazed when I look closely at it. I have a set of books where two hundred leading men have written on their part of the work in a particular branch of colloids. A great quantity of material, and so technical, all of it, on colloids alone. But when I convey to you the behavior of those two particles which are both repulsed and attracted by two forces, electrical and surface energies, that is not difficult to understand. All that colloids represent is small particles in a suspension, never at rest because of the interplay of those two energies; that is not hard to understand. The main point is that all this affects particularly the so-called "white collar" men who want to teach. They should extract from the existing sciences method, not the mere techniques. That is important for those who are specializing in education. The layman has nothing to do with special scientific techniques, and it will do him no good. You do not want the mere techniques. All you want is the method and the finished product. What you want to know is that it is being done by specialists. And, do not be too ready to criticize specialists either. They have a hard job. When you deal with reliable specialists, do not criticize them, because you are not in any position to say anything about them. And, the layman should abolish his old fashioned 'private opinions'. They are uncivilized, illegitimate, and harmful. When you deal with specialists let the views of other specialists do the criticizing. They will know what the man is talking about, that is more than you can do. That is something that the layman cannot know. When you have an honest scientific man lecturing to you, do not say you do not believe it, for you cannot disbelieve it when you don't know what you are talking about. In GS we have to trust specialists because they work under scientific control, because they deliver results; and we cannot go by private opinions which are worthless; no 'popular voting' in science.

I have just had a manuscript written by a very brilliant man who is a professor of 'philosophy' in one of the large universities here. I told you 'philosophers' cannot even understand the English of my book. This is a younger man and in a way he is partially a student of GS. It took him two years before he began to clear up a fundamental confusion of his. He mixed up direct semantic reactions, orientations, with 'logic', 'logic' as taught in schoolbooks. He still cannot get the difference between aristotelian 'logics' and aristotelian *reactions*. 'Logic' as such is defined as the 'laws of thought'; otherwise, the rules by which our 'thinking' supposedly goes. When we talk about 'thinking' as 'thinking' alone, that is elementalistic. It is not valid. The old orientations do not understand that the so-called 'logic' has very little to do with our brain processes. It is only a 'philosophical' grammar of the language we happen to use. When I speak to you I seem *coherent*, and 'logical'. Your personal relations

Lecture Fourteen

with others are often coherent though you have little or no knowledge of 'logic'. There is then such a thing as a possible theory of *coherence*. All of you here are more or less coherent. There is a place, then, for a treatise on human coherence. Such a thing has not been written yet, although it should be done. This theory of coherence would represent then the 'laws of thought', and would deal also with the structure of language. You see that the old has connected 'philosophical' grammar with the 'laws of thought'. This is foolish. And, a theory of coherence has not yet been written.

We build up a new structure of language, a *new structure*, *not* a *new language*. That new structure of language fits the structure of the world. Remember the extensional devices. They change the *structure* of the language but *not* the *language*. I want to stress that, that the extensional devices altogether *change* the *structure* of but *not* the *language*, and extensionalization changes our internal reactions. To change the language would be practically impossible. But to change the *structure* of language, is possible and simple, once we are shown *how to do it*. Then with that new extensional *structure* of language our orientations, inward reactions, follow a new extensional path. Remember you and I are not supposedly changed, but *our orientations are changing*, broadening and being made flexible and adaptable to the newer requirements of science and life. We have in the new method acquired tools that allow us to handle inwardly the manifold experiences that are becoming more and more complex, and acquire therefore a key for adjustment, and so for sanity.

The issues I am talking about are not to be evaded. Sooner or later mankind must face these facts, or cease to exist. The time seems to be remote, but great races and great cultures have appeared and disappeared the 'other day', and there are often only a few skulls left in museums. They lived on this earth, but as a race they have disappeared, because they were *not adjusted* to the conditions of living. This applies also to a great many races of animals, which have roamed this earth and have disappeared. There is nothing astonishing if we say that as a statistical probability the white race may disappear with a few skulls left eventually in museums. Perhaps a new race will begin to speculate about our skulls to find out what a sick race can do. They would say that we were maladjusted, unfit, and hence we disappeared. We are getting fit to disappear because sanity is vanishing also. The more forward we are looking, the more dangerous it looks for us. It looks as if the price of technical 'progress' is decay if we are not *inwardly* adjusted to that progress. Progress can be made constructive, provided that we know how to handle inwardly the beneficial results of the advancements of science. As you know these questions always involve a problem of method.

And the problems of 'morality' enter too, for instance. I never speak about 'morality' for the old preachings about 'morality' and 'morals' are unworkable. I want to deal with something workable. A 'mentally' ill person cannot be moral. In the beginning, a 'mentally' ill person comes to a doctor, and the first thing he does is to disclose the facts of his life, some of which may disclose factors of his illness. No matter what the patient says to the doctor, the details would not fit any old-fashioned definition of morals. The doctor will *not* 'scold'. He will not say, "be good", "be moral", etc. The doctor will pat him on the back and say, "That's all right"; psychiatrists do not preach to sick people. But he is after the causative factors in curing, not merely dealing with the symptoms, which are *undesirable* just the same. The doctor's business is to go after the *causative* factors and by doing this the symptoms disappear. In GS we do this too. Never mind the symptoms, some are disastrous, go after the causative factors. I want you to get that. We do not want certain symptoms socially or individually because some of these are dangerous and vicious. Here comes that problem: I use the term "moral" so that you will understand the need for having some sort of 'morals', using the old language. Here I stress the point that a perfectly *healthy* individual, an *adjusted* individual, *is 'moral'*! *Without any preachings* some of my students do not do certain things, simply because they do not 'fit'. Now, the problem is whether, by inquiring and by investigating, we can help the world to get being 'moral' in a workable way, and general way. The majority of you know already from your work with me, how things clear up, even with temperaments, how the degree of adjustment in mutual human relations, as well as the relations *toward ourselves* can be improved, life made happier, and some understandings built about the *mechanisms* of so-called 'morals', but in a workable way. The world cannot go on without some 'morals'; the question is, then, what theories of 'morality' have we to choose. Are they *workable* or unworkable, requiring a great metaphysical machinery to carry them out, or do we have some simple system of general sanity that brings about adjustment, sanity, and 'morality'? Have you ever seen a person 'ill'? Is he always 'sweet'? Is he, the sick Smith$_1$, *the same* when he, Smith$_1$, was healthy? That is where we stand with 'morals'. *Healthy, adjusted* people are 'moral'. Sick people are 'immoral', or even 'unmoral', having none at all! The problems of 'moral' in this world at present are important more than ever because we have discarded the old as unworkable, and nothing is left. There is no regulator for our conduct. There are no standards of evaluation by which we could orient ourselves. You can see why a new theory of evaluation is necessary. It is essential for the preservation of sanity and society. And, remember that the first attempt, by a long shot not final, of a new modern and scientific evaluation is formulated in GS This work will not stop at the present level although the breaking of the ice has been done, because at least we can compare an old method with the new. Once the second has been produced, at least we can *compare*, and *this is the basis of evaluation*. So no matter what is the final value of GS, at least we have something to compare, evaluate, and then we realize the possibility that something new may be more workable than the old, as the old has failed us. We have gotten, finally, what all sciences try to do, to formulate a set of fundamental assumptions which we can call 'postulates'.

I told you that if you are comfortable here, your comfort depends a great deal on blind faith in the architect who built this house, the men running the school, the faith that the roof will not fall on you, the floor not cave in, etc. It may seem odd to hear that your comfort depends on blind faith, but the fact is such, that assumptions are involved everywhere, and so it goes through life. I want to stress it, that everything we do, every attitude we have, involve *fundamental* rarely conscious *assumptions at the bottom*. And, do not be told by some simpleton that we can live without assumptions. Your presence and comfort here depends on many assumptions. Remember this is most serious because it is generally unknown. You would get little food at luncheon if it all had to be analyzed chemically every time you ate. That is impossible. We have to eat without that analysis, and blind faith or assumptions supplants that. Faith in the food supply, in the cook, etc., and responsibility follows from it. And, finally, we come to the control of responsibilities, such as government requirements for meats, etc. But this means distribution of control of responsibility. Here comes the role of teachers, responsibility of guidance, guidance by past achievements, guidance for the future controllers of education, etc. They are *selectors* of the problems to be taught in the schools. They are *summarizers* of the past experiences, digestors of the racial opinions, etc. They are selecting, all the time, what is best for the new generation. So, educators have great responsibilities and should have great respect. Students should treat educators well, although many educators are often *not educated* enough, and society treats them badly, too. Society treats teachers as people to be 'hired' and 'fired', to the destruction of society through the downfall of education.

You cannot spend your lifetime looking in libraries for facts, but we must depend on scientists and teachers to do that for us, then work with their revised and simplified results. Here comes the 'moral' problem again. I am finishing my lectures, and I will speak about 'morals' once more. We must have some kind of 'morals' if we are to survive. But whether they are to be workable or unworkable, *sound* in themselves, is a different proposition, and it must be based on investigation. And investigation must be based on all forms of human behavior, and mathematics and physics are forms of human behavior. They are man-made and the best available and worthy of investigation. And the moment we analyze them in action, investigate, we will find in them factors of the human 'best'. Mathematics and physics are the most perfect human achievements, and there is no doubt about that. Human behavior has built up mathematics and physics. What were then the *inside factors* of those men who built them? If we investigate the methods by which they reach their results, we will know the 'best' of human reactions. The 'best' in the humans has been crystallized in mathematics and physics. We must study the so-called 'insane'. There are evaluation problems. They would not be 'insane', if there were not. The reaction of the 'insane' are '*misevaluations*'. By a study of insanity, then, we should discover *factors of misevaluation*. We should discover factors of human evaluation at its worst. And the studying of the best of human reactions and acts, which made up the best of the sciences, and the reactions on the other side, or of the so-called 'insane' all go together. If we study these factors, we may discover factors which are constructive for a *new code* of 'morals', which may act as guidance for future generations. The old is vicious, and dangerous, because the youth, the younger generation, will not accept it. And at present, we do not have the new generally known. There are, however, principles of ethics and morals in extensionalization. When you have worked in the seminar lectures and private conferences, you should feel the benefits you have gotten. Remember too, that you have done yet very little work in it. In this class there is a student who has worked at it for years. He is not through with it, and knows that. It takes work and time to accomplish something.

Now, we are living in a new world whether we want it or not. We must have new orientations, or go under. Otherwise, laymen without the special techniques of sciences, we must be given the *method* of science. The same method that builds up the sciences has to be put into a workable form to be applicable to life. We must begin to treat our life as decently and as reasonably as any biologist treats a rat in his laboratory. We do not do that. We do not treat ourselves decently. We have not, as a rule, investigated ourselves, investigated our lives, talked about ourselves scientifically as much as a biologist has investigated his laboratory rats. We are, however, our own biologists. I am teaching you that in GS. We must have the same regard for ourselves that a biologist has toward his rats, and then we will be in a better world. I am not getting sentimental. It is better to *make* people *moral* than to *preach* ineffective 'morals'.

I will give you a shock, examine it and I challenge any 'moralist' to duplicate that example. In one of my seminars, I noticed a fine looking young man who had about an inch and a half of his tongue continually sticking out. I immediately noticed that something was wrong with him. I did not know him, but without any doubt I knew something was wrong, but I never mentioned the question of his tongue. After three weeks of the seminar that tongue disappeared, automatically. In private conferences after the seminar, it turned out that the young man represented really a group of college educated young people. I will not go into the details because they are really too horrible. I do not even tell anyone about him except saying that he lived through every 'immorality' on the docket, He had lived through them. I did not know this about him, I only noticed his tongue, which was only a symptom. I did not preach morals. When the tongue disappeared, 'immoral' impulses had disappeared with the tongue. Now suppose I had told him, "Oh, that is bad. That is 'immoral'." That would not have helped. The problem was to change the basic impulses; and we do that in psychiatry. We do not judge the symptoms, but we are after the causative factors which produce them, and when we discover them, often the symptoms may be eliminated. The difficulties developed, piled up one stratum on the other, of old prejudices, and ignorances, representing not mere ignorance, but false knowledge. We 'know' quotation marks, 'all about ourselves'. Those of you who have had private conferences with me know how much you 'know' about yourself. And what you do 'know' *happens to be false to fact*. Otherwise, you orient yourself by *false knowledge*. Imagine you do not know what is in this pocketbook, which I have in my hand. You are not unhappy about not knowing what is in it. Now, take that personally. You know I am a man and, say, you are a woman. When you do not know what is in this pocketbook, you are not unhappy. But if you 'know' that I have a letter here from your sweetheart, you would not be happy, then. False knowledge, then, is not useful. You would not be happy if you knew I had such a letter. False knowledge is often very harmful, although often *mere ignorance* is also painful. That is the point. We cannot be *merely ignorant about ourselves*, we can only have *false knowledge*, and that breeds 'insanity'. Otherwise, we must have elementary scientific knowledge about ourselves which has already been treated and embodied in GS. We supply in GS the rudiments of modern knowledge which contradicts the old false knowledge and leads to sanity.

In summarizing the course, I will start again with the fundamental *three* new *premises*, and stress that *predictability* is desirable. Predictability depends on the *similarity of structure* of our language orientations, etc., with the facts. Orientations inside may be helped or hindered by the structure of our language. We have examined the structure of our languages and have found that facts are of a non-elementalistic character, and that our languages are elementalistic. Otherwise, we began to speculate in a language not similar in structure, which makes predictability impossible. Further investigation has shown that the world in every respect consists of processes. It takes functioning, a dynamic process of electrons, to make iron, to make us, to make anything under the sun, including the sun itself. We have discovered that in a four-dimensional process world, we can have by method static cross sections, which we call events. We have discovered in a four-dimensional world, in which we live, that every point has a date and so is different at every instant; and we have also discovered that, by method, we can translate the static into dynamic, and vice versa. We can be rational, have static representations of a dynamic world; something that was not possible in the old world. We have discovered that our internal states are on unspeakable levels. The pinching of your finger is not verbal nor speakable. Even the throbbing of your sore tooth is different every instant. We have discovered the *extensional* character of the world outside our skins and inside our skins. Otherwise, the extensional character of the world which is a fact, requires an extensionalization of our orientations. We cannot otherwise handle such outside and inside worlds. We have discovered by analysis that the structure of the old languages is *intensional*. We *define* verbally a 'chair', a 'man', or whatnot. That does not fit the actual world. We have found we must use different methods. Methods which have operated for a long time in mathematics: extensional methods exhibiting the individual first, definitions next — not orientations by verbal definitions, similarities, disregarding individual differences.

For instance, define a "man", a "male", a "female", etc. We must investigate $Smith_1$, $Smith_2$, $Smith_3$, etc., empirically. We must gather *experimental data* about $Smith_1$, $Smith_2$, $Smith_3$, etc., as *given by science, inspect the data* gathered by others and form our own generalizations. Get the '*laws*' of *group behavior*. The burning of this match is a clashing of group behavior of electrons. It is a complex *group behavior of electrons*. Group behavior is different from the individual behavior. This is known even in 'psychology'. There is a complete difference between each of us, because the electrons in each of us are grouped in each differently.

So it goes with everything. To orient ourselves with any sanity in such a world we have to have a technique for extensionalizing our inside dealings, similar in structure to an extensional world

We have boiled down the old neuro-semantic and neuro-linguistic systems to some premises and have formulated the GS three premises for the new systems. The premises as you know them are: 1) that the map *is not* the territory, or a word *is not* the object or situation, 'feelings', etc. All the time *it is not*. Then we have found that the old is based on the "*is*" *of identity* which we have completely *denied* after an *investigation of the facts*. Remember the story of an aged professor of mathematics who asked me if I could deny that "every thing is identical with itself". I told him I *would deny* that an *electronic process*, a colloidal dance, etc., is ever identical with itself. He 'knew all about' electronic, colloidal, etc., theories but he had never 'thought' of this, and never applied what he supposedly 'knew'. The law of non-identity is as universal as the law of gravitation because we cannot avoid either of them. But by GS we can apply *scientific methods* boiled down to elementary fundamentals so that every layman can use it. So that is the first premise. We find that by intension we identify by the '*is*', by *intension* we have a definition, then our orientation is based on that verbalism; inside *evaluations* based on verbal definitions of *our own*. By extension we do not do that any more, but we investigate 'facts' and we *deny* this '*is*' of '*identity*'.

The *second premise* is the "*not all*". You cannot know 'all' about me. I cannot know 'all' about you. You cannot ever know 'all' about yourself or anything. And this applies everywhere. The definition by intension does not cover 'all characteristics'. That is why you have *dog*-matists and *cat*-egorists, and absolutists; they know 'all', and that by verbal *definition*, and they put down laws for 'all' time to come. Never forget the testament of a donkey. "Don't do differently than your fathers did. Do not change. What was good enough for me, is good enough for you." And the testament of Humpty Dumpty, the one who had the great fall, he would say, "*Never do as I did. Do it better.*" That is a *human* testament. In the old way we live under the 'donkey' animalistic conditions. It is about time we pass from an animal to a human level. Otherwise become extensional.

And then the *third premise* is *self-reflexiveness*, or the fact that in language we can speak *about* language. Or your words on one level will not have the same meaning on another level. You have a chapter in my book on this multiordinality or self-reflexiveness. You had better read it. I could go on for hours telling you of the messes we get into with this difficulty. Remember the barber. We cannot be honest when we deal with a trick such as this in our language. And remember we deal with much of our life on verbal levels. But if we are forewarned about the trickiness of language, we are better off. We would not have all these troubles. By chance you may have a correct solution, but by old methods we cannot have a practical solution of difficulties. Therefore, we have decided on extensionalization to help us to have a better evaluation of outside events and ourselves. Remember the formula, "I don't know, *let's see*." That means investigation, delayed reaction, etc. Think it over. In those three premises, the first

Lecture Fourteen 221

two are the *flat denial* of the old premises, and they are the only place, remember, where we can and *will not* quarrel. If you deny these, you have to deny all three, deny one, and you must deny them all. The solution of the self-reflexiveness of language on theoretical grounds is very difficult, found in the mathematical theory of types, but in GS we solve them automatically by indexes, dates, and etc. We do not need 'deep theory'. The *extensional devices do that for us*. "Never$_1$ say never$_2$" is an example.

You remember the example where you ask me if I want a smoke? The extensional *content* of my "yes$_1$" was the smoke. Do I want a drink? My "yes$_2$", then, means extensionally a drink. The "yeses" *are not* the same by extension. How can we keep them apart? *By extensional devices.* When you get into quarrels, remember that the origin of most quarrels is using one term in *different meanings*, on *different levels*, in *different orders of abstractions.* We have made some statements and the other fellow is on a different level of abstractions; we say something, but we cannot understand each other. "Get on the same level". This is done by *extensional devices. Index and date, etc., and most of our quarrels will disappear.*

To finish up, I want to summarize the most solid knowledge we have about ourselves through the use of *extensional devices.* We call them multiordinal mechanisms, which are the most solid mechanisms we have in us. They are mechanisms that go together with the multiordinal linguistic terms like: "yes", "no", "true", "false", "reality", "good", "bad", "love", "hate", etc. Much of our lives depends on these mechanisms, and use of these terms. Those terms are heavy in life. These terms are multiordinal, and they correspond to multiordinal *mechanisms* that make up our 'mentality'. By multiordinality is meant the possibility of applying a given term to different levels or orders of abstractions. Somebody makes a statement *about that statement*, otherwise a different statement using the 'same words'. Those multiordinal terms have general applicability through all levels or orders of abstractions. That is why I call them multiordinal, and on each level they have a *different extensional meaning*. The whole problem of *sanity* is *adjustment* to 'facts' and 'reality'. The problem of 'insanity' is the problem of *maladjustment*. Otherwise, sanity is impossible without getting hold of the multiordinal mechanisms; we have to show you some application of the above; the multiordinal mechanism of, for instance, "thinking *about* thinking". You can be 'thinking' about a chair, and 'thinking about the thinking' about the chair. Science and civilization are the result of multiordinal mechanisms which ultimately culminate in *consciousness of abstracting*. The whole of civilization has ultimately been built up by the multiordinal mechanisms.

That is one of the constructive categories of multiordinality. Now I will show you another mechanism where the undesirable characteristics are reversed by the consciousness that the mechanisms are multiordinal. For example, take first order 'hate', first order 'doubt'. You are not a pleasant person to live with if you have *first order doubt* or *first order hate*. But, when you pass to a *second order doubt* or *hate*, that is if you hate hate, and doubt doubt, then the effects are reversed. When you doubt your first order doubt, then you have

Lecture Fourteen

abolished your first order doubt. You have become scientifically conscious of the mechanism, and *cautious*. Second order hate always hates first order hate. It is close to 'love'. In life this is constructive. That is the second category of multiordinality, exhibiting second order mechanisms that are reversing the first order mechanisms.

The third is found in psychology. That is, worry about worry, etc. Often when they bring patients to psychiatrists, they are in a bad shape. And they worry about their worries and often they go 'insane'. In the hospitals they merely explain in different words that first order worry may be legiti-mate, but the second order worry is not, and in a few weeks, often the patient snaps out of it. So we have those three categories. I want to show you an application of the above to everyday life. There are a great many elements of 'ethics' and 'morality', etc., involved in this. I will speak in a rather 'polite language' and you must add your imagination to that. Do you and I have a bargain then? Speaking about 'morals', 'sex behavior', etc., *imagine* that you *indulge* in something harmful, say you like to *eat matches*; I really mean much more than that. I will speak about 'eating matches', but I mean the deepest 'moral' issues. Imagine *you like* to 'eat matches'. That is not healthy, but you like it, so you eat them. Now I am $Smith_1$ not myself, but $Smith_1$, a preacher, and I tell you, "Oh that is immoral. Not good", and so on, and so on. "You will not go to Heaven", etc. And your answer to yourself and to me, "Oh, I don't believe it. I don't believe your old bunk." That is really what you will say, if you like 'eating matches', and I begin to preach 'morals' to you. Now, here comes a problem, if you say so, you will keep on 'eating matches'; you have *dismissed* me and my 'wisdom' for good. You dismissed me and *my help* for good, and *without my help* you would keep on eating the harmful matches. That would not be good for you. You would finally pay the price. Now that is a picture of the old. Now GS comes in. That means extensionalization, knowing about multiordinal mechanisms, etc. The situation is not changed. You still like to 'eat matches' which is not good for you. I know that, not as Smith$_1$, a preacher, this time, but as a general semantician and I am interested in you, and I speak to you about 'eating matches', in terms of *the new*, not *the old*, in *terms of evaluation*. You, by habit, would dismiss me in the same old way. Do you know what I would say? "*Is that so?. Your lack of evaluation is evaluation of a low order*. And, dismiss that if you can." You cannot dismiss that for your *lack of evaluation is only evaluation of a lower order*. Otherwise, you cannot dismiss multiordinal terms. It gets under your skin and you begin to chew upon it. The old, you can dismiss and forget, but a multiordinal evaluation, you cannot dismiss. It will bother you until you begin to see what happens. This is the way of using 'evaluation'; multiordinal mechanisms work in this way. *Are you getting that?* Another thing which has been and still is a great difficulty and in a way is tragic, is the question of 'sex' maladjustment and misunderstanding of 'sex'. Remember the 9/10 and the 1/10 working of the gonads. This is a neuro-physiological fact that they are *energy-producing* glands all over the body, brain included, therefore, we must recognize that. We have to revise our old orientations on the 'sex' subject because the old has not taken into account the 9/10 functioning. On certain levels *biological* forces work unhampered, say on the *level of animals*. *Not so with us*. Our *biological* levels can be *twisted* by *semantic levels of evaluation*. Project the 9/10 on the 1/10, and you have *too little energy where it is needed*, and *too much energy* in the 1/10, or proper 'sex functions'. Animals cannot do that because they do not have semantic mechanisms. Often this ends in asylums. Always it is 'immoral'. On the white level we must have a *new attitude* towards each other and towards ourselves. On the animal level the 'first order enjoyment' depends on the enjoyment of the 1/10, but on the white human level we must go beyond that to the second order enjoyment, namely the enjoyment of the enjoyment. That is the working of the organism-as-a-whole. Topology comes in here.

Well, I suppose this review may have very practical results and applications, but again I must repeat that it takes months to be extensionalized, and only by getting extensionalized do we reach results, positive constructive results. So the whole aim of *Science and Sanity* and GS is to train us to extract from science the factors which have made it, and thus help us to discover *factors of sanity*. We do not need to have great 'scientific knowledge' or to be a 'great scientist' to abstract the techniques of science. *Extract the methods* and the results will follow, as experience shows. That is the aim of GS. I have enjoyed working with you. Thank you.

SUPPLEMENT

A SEMANTIC INTERPRETATION OF THE FUNDAMENTAL VALUES IN THE STUDY OF FOREIGN LANGUAGES

President Brewer asked me to say a few words about the attitude, which follows from general semantics, toward the study of *foreign languages*. Semantically it is rather an important problem. We must discriminate sharply between the study of *antique dead languages* such as Latin or Greek, which are indispensable for some future specialists, but semantically unimportant; and the study of *modern languages*, at least *one* modern foreign language, which is of *utmost semantic importance*.

It must be granted that the study of foreign languages is at least tedious. However for *cultural development* it is desirable that we should travel and know more about the world than our own little native village or country. Travel with ignorance of foreign languages, at least French, is often *irritating* and does not bring the beneficial results which should be expected. If you speak only English or 'American' you will be *tied up* with hotels and 'tourist houses' where English or 'American' is understood, but you will *learn* very little about a new type of life which people in other countries live. In other words, the main benefit you *could get* out of your travel would be lost, and your 'private opinions' about other countries and their human lives, would remain small village, silly, and *sometimes vicious gos-*

sips. The opinions of silly 'Americans' who do not speak some foreign language, yet try to travel are just as *ridiculous* as the opinions of silly men who do *not speak English or 'American'* and travel, say, in the United States. As a rule they have not *understood anything* about what they have seen and return 'home' more *petty* and silly than they started off their 'travel' to 'learn something culturally'.

I was speaking about *practical*, rather superficial cultural issues until now, yet the *semantic serious benefits* of studying foreign languages, go much further. They affect directly that *supreme* aim of *extensionalization*, which I call "consciousness of abstracting". Thus if through the *knowledge* of a foreign language you know that what you call "cane" in English or 'American' is called "laska" in Polish; or what you call "love" in Anglo-American is called "amour" in French, etc., this would have a profound semantic effect on your orientations helping the consciousness of abstracting, that words *are not* the things we are *talking* about, as talking remains talking, and 'facts', things, etc., are not verbiage. If a few of you will 'think' this over, you would be closer to consciousness of abstracting, and so further on the road toward extensionalization, and so, *on your road toward sanity*.

So it seems that the study of foreign languages is culturally and semantically very important, and in spite of its tediousness, a *profitable enterprise*.

I am sending you off as a very cooperative dear class, with my best wishes for your individual best adjustment, which can be achieved if *you work hard enough*, without which you, and I, have only *wasted time*. Well dear class, best luck and good night.

Addendum for 1964 Edition

Olivet, Michigan
June 21, 1937

Count Alfred Korzybski
Dearborn Plaza Hotel
1032 N. Dearborn
Chicago, Illinois

My dear Count Alfred Korzybski:

    The Board of Trustees of Olivet College has asked me to thank you on their behalf for the fine and generous service which you have rendered the College in conducting seminars and conferences in General Semantics here during the past eight weeks. They feel that your work has been a significant contribution to the College, and they anticipate that its effects will be far-reaching, not alone amongst the individuals with whom you have worked, but as it will be reflected in the educational program of the College. They realize that you have done this work at considerable personal sacrifice to yourself, and they want you to know that they are deeply grateful to you for it.

    Please accept my personal thanks and best wishes as well as those of the Board.

Yours ever sincerely,

Joseph Brewer
President of Olivet College

JB:A

Olivet, Michigan
23 June 1937

Count Alfred Korzybski
Dearborn Plaza Hotel
1032 N. Dearborn
Chicago, Illinois

Dear Count Alfred Korzybski:

I want to thank you most whole-heartedly for the splendid work you have done here in the course of the past two months through the fourteen lectures in General Semantics which you conducted and the private conferences which you afforded the members of the seminar. It's difficult for me to estimate the value of this work in the individuals and to the school since the results will, I know, continue to appear for a long time to come.

Two years ago, when you were here for a shorter time and delivered some introductory lectures, you set a yeast going in the College which has continued to ferment. The results of that were seen clearly in the attendance at the seminar and the developing interest amongst members of the Faculty who were here for the earlier lectures.

As you know, there were altogether over one hundred members of the College who attended the lectures. Out of a student body of two hundred and sixty and a Faculty of thirty-five, I feel that this was a good proportion since the whole thing was on a voluntary basis and done at a particularly busy time of year. The whole College has been aroused by the lectures, and I think we are well on the way to establishing a non-Aristotelian orientation for all our work here.

Your work in consultation with members of the Faculty, looking towards this, has been particularly helpful and plans for work along the lines which you suggested are going forward this summer.

The immediate results of the seminar and conferences are to be seen clearly in individual cases. As a worker in experimental natural science, we have looked to see you "produce the goods". The results of your direct retraining of the nervous system in individual members of the seminar have been obvious and clear. My colleagues and I have watched the changes happen and are expecting to see further results as the work goes on here.

In the case of a number of students, three young women in particular, we have seen a general adjustment to life and a growing maturity; in two other cases this development has been very marked indeed. Before our very eyes these young women have matured, developed balance, and have appeared quite transformed. Another young woman not only has matured noticeably but has overcome a great deal of unhappiness in her own life. From being a girl who apparently "brooded" a good deal, she has become lively and cheerful and beautifully balanced.

One young man, a good student, had a curious "lifelessness" about him. Through his work with you he has quite definitely come to life, and appears a different person. One young woman who was very artificial in her manner has become ever so much more natural. One of your old students from the Chicago seminars has made a further advance and has made a further improvement in her work.

One very talented young man who seemed always to be working under great tension has slowed down noticeably and his work is showing the result of this relaxation. A number of other students have been generally toned up and put more squarely on their feet in regard to both their private and vocational problems. These are all the "average" cases. A number of quite extraordinary things have happened. One young man who had worried a good deal with sex troubles found them all cleared up in a few moments by your discussion of the one-tenth — nine-tenths functioning of the gonads. This in turn straightened out other confusions and difficulties for him.

One member of the Faculty, who has had a very complicated set of difficulties is quite obviously getting hold of himself as a result of your training. Another member of the Faculty who has had from early childhood a very serious and extraordinary difficulty has been almost completely released from it and will undoubtedly be entirely free before long.

In at least three cases you discovered that there were serious difficulties deriving from the fact that normally left-handed people had been forced to use their right hands as children. The process of going back to the left hand and the understanding which you gave them of the mechanisms involved in this has done perfectly extraordinary things to clear up their difficulties.

One young woman who was very tense and had a speech difficulty is now quite relaxed and her speech has cleared up considerably as a result of the shift. Another young woman who was also very tense has relaxed greatly.

The most extraordinary case of this sort is probably that of Mr. —, whose own report I am attaching to this letter. Since this letter was written Mr. — has continued to improve. The examinations which he wrote at the end of the year were hardly comparable to his earlier papers. Not only was his hand-writing legible, but his material was well organized and his expression thoroughly coherent. None of these things had been true of his work previously. His speech has cleared quite phenomenally.

Perhaps the most extraordinary case of all is one of apparent homo-sexuality, in which all the active symptoms were positive. Your analysis revealed that this was merely a substitute for masturbation, and with the consciousness of the mechanism which you gave this student the homo-sexuality completely disappeared and positive hetero-sexuality was established. This has been further confirmed to me by him since you left Olivet.

In these very tangible results we have seen the value of General Semantics and extensional orientation. In many small ways, too, I have seen it working right through the College. To my mind the great importance of your work for us here has inhered, however, not alone in the actual cases with which you have dealt and in which you have affected so much, but in the impetus you have given to us all to work constructively not only for ourselves but for the building up of the extensional attitude throughout the work of the institution.. We are convinced that by so doing we shall not only promote happiness in individual lives, but shall see much better work done academically in the College as a result of continued training.

When I say "we" all the way through, I include myself and those of my colleagues on the Faculty whom you know and whom you know to be particularly convinced and sympathetic. I do not want to imply that the whole Faculty is in accord with these views. I think it is safe to say, however, that the majority is, and I can assure you that my ambition is to bring the whole group around so that the College as a whole can function in a non-Aristotelian orientation.

I want to say now just a word in regard to your own presentation in the lectures. You had here one of the most difficult possible teaching situations. You had a very large class mixed both as to sex and age. You had both men and women and the age range was from sixteen to sixty-five. To handle a group like this is a feat, and you did it extraordinarily well. What impressed me particularly was your ability to watch everybody in the class at the same time, to stop when necessary to clarify the presentation for individuals, and the general effectiveness of the presentation for all concerned.

Your own delivery has improved since your lectures here two years ago and you have improved in the organization and presentation of your materials. Your many new examples are striking and your use of them impressive. The only criticisms I heard were on the part of a few members of the seminar who used probably as an excuse for their own shortcomings the complaint that you sometimes repeated the same idea in the same form too often or that you spent time saying what great things General Semantics would accomplish which might have been spent to greater advantage in getting on with the exposition of General Semantics. I myself did not feel this nor I think did any but a very small portion of the group. Repetition and drill are essential to understanding General Semantics and it is necessary to emphasize constantly the importance of applying General Semantics rather than merely accepting it. The times, however, when the class itself through its responsiveness permitted you to be most meaty and least "gossipy" were the times when you yourself were happiest and when the class was most enthusiastic. Altogether it was a most effective and impressive presentation of extremely difficult material.

Once more let me thank you whole-heartedly for all you have done for us and express the hope that you will come back frequently to keep us on the track and help us carry on.

With every good wish, I am

>Yours sincerely,
>
>Joseph Brewer
>President of Olivet College
>Olivet, Michigan

JB:A